UBER & OUT 2

More Tales from the World of an Uber Driver

by

Walter Anthony Barringer Dinteman

© 2018, 2019

Uber & Out 2

Kirkland Press

ISBN-13: 978-708212094

Acknowledgements

First, I'd like to thank my Uber driving colleagues who contributed some of my favorite stories although most of them are my own. I also must say that the stories are true with names changed to protect the innocent, or guilty, as the case may be.

I want to thank some of the 40,000 riders I have had over the past five years who encouraged this project not only with stories of their own, but with the words every author likes to hear, "I will buy that book!"

For factual information, I must thank Uber, Inc. and Lyft, Inc. for things pertaining to their operations, driver requirements, etc. but I make no claim as to the currency of that information as things do change over time. For any errors on my part, I apologize for any misunderstandings on my part.

Lastly, I want to thank my friends, Chris Lowry and Kevin Borgersen, both Uber drivers, and also Doug Mason, a fellow writer, for their encouragement.

Preface

In November 2014 I signed up to be an Uber driver in Asheville, North Carolina. I became a "Partner" as Uber calls its drivers. I had retired from a forty-year career in the publishing industry. After trying several various retirement jobs, I found Uber to be the most interesting one of all. In retirement, I really enjoy this job with no schedule and no immediate supervisor, it is, basically, an "all carrots, no sticks" work environment. One prerequisite of the job that Uber does not emphasize enough is that one should really like to drive. It helps, of course, if you also like people. In my case, both are true. Having done ten thousand trips and having at least 30,000 people in my car, it had better be true that I like driving and people!

Uber & Out captures some of the lighter, and darker, moments of my three year's experience, mainly in Asheville, North Carolina. That town of 90,000, with 425,000 in the greater metropolitan area, has become a Mecca for tourists (12M last year) as well as being a top retirement destination. For that reason, Uber has found a perfect place to do the business of ride sharing. On weekends, drivers from East Tennessee and Upstate South Carolina also come to join Asheville drivers to facilitate the movement of thousands of people. They drive people (in Uber jargon "PAX") around town, in and out of the suburbs, airport, Biltmore House, 200+ hotels, 800+ restaurants, and the dozens of breweries and scores of music and wedding venues. Last I heard, Asheville was the 6th largest destination in the USA for wedding venues located in grand hotels, picturesque farms, and mountain vistas. The Biltmore House alone has hosted more than a dozen weddings in a single day! Little wonder then that wedding related rides alone constitute as much as a quarter of my rides from May to October.

Since I drive primarily at night, safe to say, most of my trips are alcohol related. Asheville has several times been recognized as "Beer City USA." Most of the 30+ breweries are small craft brewing operations, but there are some giants as well with Sierra Nevada and New Belgium's East Coast facilities being very big tourist destination themselves.

I have also included some comments on Uber and advice about being an Uber driver if you may be considering that.

A word to parents: Some of these stories are, shall I say, "R-rated." So, share with youngsters if you want, but caution is advised.

One welcome aspect of being an Uber driver is the regular opportunity to observe a great number of people mostly being themselves and revealing the humor and pathos that make us humans the wonderful beings that we are. What follows are vignettes describing some of the more bizarre and memorable trips that I and my colleagues have witnessed on the road over the past several years. Perhaps you will recognize yourself among the stories and characters presented here. Enjoy!

Preface to the Second Edition

In the year and some months since *Uber & Out* was published, I have continued to drive for both Uber and Lyft except for three months when both companies decided to fire me. Well, "deactivate your account" as they like to phrase it. See story about that below.

Every few weeks I get more stories, bizarre instances, crazy sightings, and some pretty crazy people in my car. Thus the experience begged for a new edition which retains the best of the old ones, some updated, as well as twenty entirely new tales. As I tell my riders, "The stories are true; I have only changed the names of the guilty."

"That's Asheville!"

Years ago, Asheville borrowed, or stole, a bumper sticker slogan from Austin, Texas. "Keep Austin Weird!" became "Keep Asheville Weird!" and the people here have to do their best to do just that.

When anything weird is seen, which elsewhere would be regarded as abnormal or bizarre, locals and tourists alike shrug their shoulders and simply say, "That's Asheville!"

Here are a couple of examples of what I mean that indeed keeps Asheville weird:

A young blond woman in dreadlocks, guitar strapped to her back was cruising along a busy street on a skateboard. Now, that alone is not weird enough to illicit a "That's Asheville!" comment. But the fact that she had a border collie on a leash towing her does make the "That's Asheville" threshold.

The Lazoom comedy tour bus also qualifies for "That's Asheville!" in and of itself; but also for having a hairy chested guy

in a nuns habit riding a 'penny farthing'
bicycle through town to promote Lazoom tours.

Speaking of weirdness on bicycle,
I was Ubering along Asheville's main street
when I saw a young man dressed as Marge
Simpson. He had a perfect blue beehive
hairdo but with small twinkling white lights
woven into his doo.

Not long ago, my Uber
passengers and I spotted a white delivery van
behind Ben's Tune Up. It had a logo cartoon of
a man with a blowtorch. The business sign
read, "Asheville Mobile Welding and Tattoo
Removal Service." In smaller letters you could
read that the van actually was used by
Asheville Brewing Company next door to Ben's.

Ben's Tune Up, formerly a
garage for car repairs, now a popular bar has
recently began brewing, but not beer, just saki.
Try the jalapeno-pineapple saki. Now, "That's
Asheville!"

Naked in the Night

On a fairly long trip, a twenty miler, to the rural mountains north of Asheville, a female rider asked, "What were your wildest and craziest trips?"

"Well, I do have some among the thousands of trips I have made." I went on to tell her some of the stories you will read of in this book.

As we rounded a mountain turn, the woman exclaimed, "Oh, my God! There's a naked man walking!"

"Jeez, you're right!" I agreed, slowing enough to see that except for a sturdy pair of walking boots, the man was absolutely "buck naked."

I said to the PAX, "I guess you can say this was one of the wilder things I have seen."

I went on up the mountain to her home, laughing and speculating all the way as to what it was we had just witnessed.

On the way back, now about half a mile farther down the slope, I saw the man again. I thought about speaking to him, but then decided just to wave. He waved back as if his naked stroll at 1:00 AM was just a normal part of his nightly routine on a warm summer night near Burnsville.

Naked in the Night 2

On another summer sight, about 12:30 AM, I approached the roundabout on Haywood Rd in the River Arts District, home to hundreds of artists in all media. There, in the center of the roundabout, was a woman flashing her naked body with a shawl and holding an open umbrella.

Instead of if just driving around on my way which would be normal with the often stated comment "That's just Asheville!" But since I wasn't on an Uber trip, I stopped to ask if she were OK.

"I am protesting!" she replied.

"What are you protesting?" I inquired.

"Duke Power."

Duke Power, a.k.a. Progress Energy, is a regular punching bag for environmental activists. "So what did they do this time?" I had to know.

"They bought Phil Mechanic's (art studio building) and all the artists are

13

going to be kicked out." I later learned that the property was going to be an electric power sub-station.

"Well, good for you! I hope your protest succeeds."

Last I heard, the sub-station was located elsewhere, or put on hold. It occurred to me that had she just been holding a sign, nobody would know or care about artists being kicked out of a building.

Lesson: Next time you want to protest something, take off all your clothes, grab a shawl and your umbrella and stand on a street corner. That would be much more effective than just holding a sign.

The Missing Bachelor

I had a wedding planner as a passenger one night who told me that a recent edition of his professional journal had a cover feature on Asheville. They said that Asheville and the surrounding mountains were venues that make the area the sixth most popular wedding destination in the USA.

I can certainly believe that with up to 25% of all my trips from April-October being in some ways being wedding related. Not surprising that some of the crazier stories are also "wedding related."

Jake, fellow Uber driver I know had picked up a large group of inebriated young men who were members of a wedding party. The Uber vehicle was designated "Uber XL" like a Chevy Suburban with three back rows.

Jake took everyone, so he thought, to a huge AirBnB in the mountains south of town. He dropped them off and went on his way, picking up and letting off a dozen or more people on several short rides around town.

Two hours later in downtown Asheville, while the driver was perched waiting for ride request, a head popped up from the third row seat.

A young man, shouted, "Where, the fuck, am I?"

Jake responded, "Who the fuck are you?" The answer was that he was from that wedding party dropped off at the AirBnB cabin some two hours earlier!

Apparently nobody in the wedding party noticed Bob's absence nor did any of the subsequent riders see, hear, or smell the passed out man on the back seat.

Of course Jake got Bob out to his original destination; the missing bachelor now restored to the party.

Get Me Outta Here!

A couple of years ago, I picked up a young guy coming out of the Universal Joint, a bar and restaurant on Haywood Rd. That West Asheville strip is one of the most popular places to visit in Asheville featuring, bars, breweries, music venues and some very fine restaurants.

"Get me outta here as soon as possible!" Jason yelled as he got in my car. I noticed he had not entered a destination, so I asked "So where are we going, Jason?"

"It doesn't matter! Just drive!" And so I did. Soon I noticed a white SUV following us.

"Do you know there's a white SUV following us?" I asked.

"Yes! She's crazy! Just drive!" Jason cried. At first I was intrigued by the thought of a Hollywood style escape where the hero tries to lose the bad guys. I sped up exceeding the speed limit on Haywood Road. She stayed right behind.

"Turn here!" Jason yelled. I did. I then came to my senses and realized that those Hollywood chases usually end in a crash. It also occurred to me that she and I would most likely get pulled over by the police for various motor vehicle violations so my next tactic was to annoy her by driving very slowly; like 5 mph. We covered miles of side streets on both sides of the main drag.

After 15 minutes of this nonsense I drove into a convenience store and rolled down my window. She pulled up alongside, rolled her window down and shouted. "Tell my boyfriend to get out of that car right now!"

Without a word, the boyfriend did as he was commanded and climbed into her car. I ended the trip which was fairly pricy considering the whole convoluted ride was less than a mile from where it began.

Since Uber's database collects and keeps the Google map record of every single trip, I was a little concerned that this particular trip would appear as a "run around" by a crooked driver trying to up his fare. Well, that never happened I was relieved to learn.

I am Soooo Tired!

A woman named Rachel made an Uber request from a popular bar for her friend Tim, saying, "He's a lot of fun, just take him home, please."

Tim was at Ben's Tune-Up, a former garage, now bar and saki brewery. Tim came outside at 11:00 PM which is relatively early for most patrons of bars here.

Tim appeared, looking very much like Frank Zappa, long curly black hair and a heavy mustache. He had on a pair of ripped jeans and you could see pink tights showing through the tears on each thigh.

Tim got in the front seat and said, "Thanks for taking me, I am soooo tired!"

"Have you been working hard?" I asked.

"Yes I have, and I haven't had a break in two weeks."

"Oh, really? What do you do?"

"I have five jobs." Tim said matter-of-factly.

"Wow!" I said, "What are those jobs?

"I'm a stripper at bachelorette parties. That's one. I also am a flame dancer. Girls like that."

"Flame dancer?"

"Yes." Tim replied, "I twirl flaming batons for parties. It's very popular.

"Sounds dangerous." I commented.

"Well, that's not as dangerous as being a referee for kick ball."

"What's dangerous about being a referee for a kid's game? Do you get paid for that?"

"No, it's the Asheville Adult Kick Ball League. I do get paid. One day the guys on one team said I made a bad call. The threatened to kill me! And another time both teams were fighting and I had to call the police. Yes, kick ball can be dangerous!"

"So what else do you do, Tim?"

"I book acts for an Asheville music venue. That's really my main job. Then I work there as a bartender and sometimes, like this week, as a security guard."

I drove Tim up an icy mountain road still in the city limits and GPS showed I had arrived. The point was beside a gigantic oak tree.

"I live in that tree." Tim said with a straight face.

"Really?"

"No, I'm screwing with you, but everything else is true and I am soooo tired and glad to be home... behind this tree."

The Great Inventor

One very late night I picked up an exceedingly drunk young man at a rural apartment building in Swannanoa, NC. He wanted to be taken to his girlfriend's apartment in a housing project in West Asheville. I know of drivers who refuse to drive in there due to the high crime rate including a few murders in the past year. I will go anyway because I don't believe in prejudging those places or the people who live there.

But it was 2:00 AM and my rider, Sam, was having second thoughts about going over there himself. Once we were on Interstate 40, he started to tell me about his "great invention." Sam, was not only an avid beer drinker, he was very much into recycling his beer cans. Instead of mashing them flat and putting them into black garbage bags, Sam had a better idea: He took several wooden pallets, broke them down, and built a framework that would fit in the back of his pick-up truck. Then he said he stapled chicken wire to make a good sized cage for his voluminous stash of beer cans. Driving on the highway this night refreshed his memory of the trip to the recycling center.

"I had a real good load, about $80 worth." Sam recalled. "Then I headed out 40 to the recycling center. About a mile after getting on the highway, I seen cans flying out of the chicken-wire cage. Before I could pull over damn near every one of 'em had blowed out on the highway. It took me an hour to get those bastards back in the cage! I still think it was a good invention; I just didn't fasten the top well enough. And I was right about the weight and I did get all the cans back, but when I got to the recycle station, they told me that the price of aluminum had gone down and the sons-a-bitches would only give me fifty dollars."

We were soon at the projects. Sam again said he didn't know if this was a good idea. But he got out in the well-lit parking lot. I thought that this was perhaps not as good an idea as the chicken-wire beer can recycling cage.

I waited until he had gone safely inside his friend's apartment.

The Sweetest Bride

As mentioned earlier, Asheville is a destination for thousands of weddings each year. Occasionally, I felt that I was part of the festivities or the wedding party itself. One night a wedding planner had called an Uber to deliver the bride and groom to a honeymoon hideaway in the nearby mountains.

The bride could not have been more beautiful, a dark-eyed brunette in a perfect white gown her head topped in a wedding hat that looked more like the halo of an angel. In contrast the red-headed, blue-eyed, groom was pale white; stiff in his unaccustomed tuxedo. His expression appeared to be one of sheer terror.

I had the Whitney Houston song *I Will Always Love You* playing through my Pandora app. The bride began singing along in the softest sweetest voice you've ever heard. The groom was unsmiling like a prisoner being led to the gallows.

This scene was so intensely sweet it brought a tear to my eyes. They were the perfect virgins, on the brink of the rest of their lives. I was happy to be a small part of it.

Assault on a Female

It was only a couple of weeks after my encounter with the "sweetest bride" that I happened to be the driver for a couple involved in a heated argument. They were also coming from a wedding celebration.

Apparently the male partner of the young woman had taken great offense at something that was said or implied by his lady friend. He began to shout obscenities. "You bitch. You whore!" he screamed. We were just a few blocks from their destination, an AirBnB in West Asheville. Then he grabbed her arm.

"Stop grabbing my arm. You're hurting me!" Krista yelled.

"Hey, calm down back there!" I said rather loudly.

"You shut the fuck up!" Her date replied to me. I pulled over to the curb an ordered the couple out. Both got out. She began to walk briskly away. He grabbed Krista and threw her up against the side of a brick building.

I rolled down my window and shouted, "I'm calling the cops!"

He let her go and she walked rapidly away. Some people from a nearby bar who were standing on the street smoking said they had seen what happened and one said, "Good! Call the cops."

When she was about a block away, I rolled up near her and asked if she were ok. I did call 911 to report the assault.

"Yeah. I'm close to the house and I have the Airbnb key." Krista replied

I don't know what happened after that, but in North Carolina, "Assault on a Female" is a serious crime as it should be.

Gun Control or the Lack Thereof

Speaking of assault on a female, one of my last trips before sending this book off to the publisher involved just that.

I picked up Archie at the County Detention Center where he had just served a pre-trial stay in jail for assault on his girlfriend.

On the way to Sherri's apartment (the scene of the alleged crime), Archie told me a rambling tale that began. "I have the right to carry a gun."

I agreed that most Americans do have that right. I asked him, "Archie, why do you have a gun?"

"I don't know, I guess it's because I have always had guns. I was in the Army and I was an MP for six years."

"So," I replied, "You just feel more comfortable with having guns?"

"Yeah carrying a gun makes me feel safe."

"Well then, what happened to get you in jail?"

"I had my guns laid out on the floor and Sherri was pissed off and said, 'Why don't you just take a bullet.' I picked up my pistol and she screamed and ran out of the house."

"Golly, then what happened?"

"Some asshole neighbor called the cops when they seen my gun. I had it stuck in the top of my pants. I have the right to carry a gun if it ain't concealed."

"When the SWAT team come they told me to raise my hands and that made my shirt cover my gun. They said I had a concealed weapon and threw me on the ground."

I asked Archie, "Why did you follow Sherri outside with a gun stuck in your pants? Did that make you feel safer?" Archie had no reply. Just a blank stare that said he really didn't know.

I told Archie that I had a concealed carry permit. I got that to find out how difficult and comprehensive the background checks were in North Carolina. Now, I don't carry a gun and never want to, but I can say that if every gun owner had to pass a background check such as the one in North Carolina, that is just about all the gun control we need.

Archie is a poster child for the need for more gun control: He told me that on the day the incident happened he had "blacked out" at his job at the Veterans Administration Hospital where he worked as an orderly.

He said, "I don't remember anything I did that Friday before I blacked out. They said I had to go on paid leave and they would try to get me on disability. Said I had PTSD. I guess I do."

Archie then got on his phone with Sherri. "Sherri, I swear I'm OK, but I need to come home. I got nowhere else to stay."

Sherri also told Archie that she tried to tell the judge that the whole incident was a "misunderstanding." She went on to tell the judge, "You shouldn't bring charges against Archie, but the judge said he had to go by my (original) written statement that I was threatened."

When he hung up with Sherri, Archie said he thought he could beat that concealed carry charge. "I am going to get my conceal carry in three months. That makes it enough time since I had a DUI which is a year."

I have trust in the system for keeping concealed guns from Archie. In truth, Archie shouldn't have any guns at all.

When he got out of the car, Sherri apparently permitted Archie to come back home. Still hope she's okay.

Guns and Uber

Uber has a "no weapons" policy for drivers, but I'm not sure about riders. I never ask a passenger if they are armed or not.

There are very rare cases of Uber drivers being assaulted or shot, but, of course, when that happens it makes world-wide news. Recently, a rider assaulted a driver with a knife. That particular driver did have a gun and he shot the passenger to death.

Comments on our local Uber Driver Face Book page included one that advocated that Uber allow drivers to carry guns.

I responded that I thought that was a very bad idea. First, what would that mean? A loaded and cocked pistol at the ready at all times? If a passenger in the back seat pulls a gun to rob you, would he wait for you to get yours before he shot you? Other scenarios are as unlikely as that to have a positive outcome.

Sure, maybe just having a gun in the car makes a person with an anxiety syndrome feel more comfortable like Archie in the last story.

Another point: taxicab drivers in many cities are sitting ducks for robbery or worse. That's because most of their transactions are in cash and the perps know it. But Uber drivers deal in credit card transactions and typically have little cash and, I think, the perps know it.

Horny Passenger

I make it a rule not to comment on the appearance of any passengers unless they ask, "How do I look?" So no matter how beautiful, cool or bizarre someone may appear, I just keep quiet.

In Asheville, one of the most favorite holidays is Halloween. When October 31st does not fall on a weekend, the costumes, parties, and bar and house decorations appear days before and after that date. In general, people in Asheville will jump on many other holidays or just random times to take the opportunity to get into costume.

An Asheville tradition for a decade is the Zombie Walk. Like creatures from the Living Dead, people with blackened eyes, grey faces, and ragged clothing walk stiff legged a mile from North Asheville to downtown. This event happens about a month before Halloween. In 2008, the Zombie Walk came on the same day as an appearance by then Vice Presidential Candidate Sarah Palin. It was a surreal scene when the Zombies came marching past the Civic Center where the candidate was speaking. Palin supporters, protestors, and zombies milled about in the streets shouting, arguing, or just moaning.

I say this as a back story to say that you never know what kind of person or character you might get on an Uber ride in this town. So, one evening a guy with a red makeup face got in. He had a shaven head, but had retained two large tufts of hair which he had waxed heavily into pointed devil horns on both sides of his scalp. He appeared to be a very realistic Satan and pretty scary. That is, if you believe in the Devil and I don't, so I was OK. His friend also had a shaven head. His was adorned with black and purple polka-dots.

This was on a night about three months before Halloween. I said nothing about their appearance. Just gave them the normal greeting. "Hey, George, so where are we going?" I always say the name of the PAX and their destination to confirm the request.

"Scandals." That was the correct answer; the most popular disco in Asheville and one where the bizarre is the norm.

Halloween Favorites

Halloween is not only Asheville's favorite celebration it is by far the busiest week I have Uber driving. Every year there are very creative costumes as one would expect in a town that embraces the counter culture, arts, and creativity in general.

My personal favorites over the past several years:

I had two human bananas in my car. The couple barely fit in the backseat; the fruits were so large; little smiling faces showing at the sides.

But they were relatively small compared to the T-Rex that made me concerned about visibility and the chance that the inflatable dinosaur costume might explode as we drove to a Halloween party.

Every Halloween many women choose to be either cheer leaders or hookers; the latter being the single most popular fantasy in Asheville. Amongst the cheerleaders, was one slightly overweight, hairy-chested male. He would have been pretty funny all by himself,

but he was accompanied hand-in-hand by a
hippie who evoked the popular portrait of
Jesus Christ if you think a Day-Glo Jesus
painted on velvet is the most accurate
depiction of The Savior.

Where's My House?

I drive mainly at night so it is not uncommon, rather the norm, to have passengers who have been drinking. In fact as you will note in this book, many of the stories are "alcohol related."

Such was the time at 2 AM when I arrived at a pick-up spot only to find no one there. The restaurant on the request had been closed for three hours. Since Uber has the feature that allows a driver to call the person who requested the ride, I called Renee. Renee didn't answer, but a man did, "This is Paul, I'm with Renee."

"Well Paul you apparently aren't at Limones Restaurant. So where are you?"

"Uh, Ok, we are at the Twisted Laurel."

"Alright that's only a couple of blocks from here. I'm on my way."

When I arrived at the Twisted Laurel restaurant and bar there was a middle aged couple enjoying a passionate kiss under a street lamp. It was sort of a scene from a 1940's romantic movie. I guessed correctly that would be Paul with a receding hairline and Renee with bright red hair.

As they got in the car I could see immediately why the pick-up address was wrong and that Paul had to take my call. Renee, as the expression goes was "three sheets to the wind."

I started the ride to a destination in Oakley, a neighborhood in East Asheville. I had heard Renee say "Yep!" when I gave the address.

As soon as I got on the highway, Renee complained, "This ishint the way to my housh!"

"Well, I'm just following my GPS directions. Could be wrong, I suppose."

"This is wrong!" Renee insisted.

"Paul, are we going the right way?" I asked the more sober of the couple.

"I don't know. I have never been there! I just met Renee."

With that non-information I proceeded to the destination relying on GPS navigation.

"This isn't right!" Renee kept saying. I kept driving.

I got off I-240 at exit 8 for Fairview Road in Oakley. Then I drove on down that road to the designated street and to the designated address clearly visible from the street.

"We're here according to GPS." I said looking at the huge wooden numbers on the house.

"Where's my house?" Renee said.

"So, that *isn't* your house?" I asked.

"I don't know. Is this it, Renee?" Paul asked his new friend.

"Oh, yeah that's it." Renee confirmed that she was indeed in front of her own house!

The couple left the car, then Paul asked, "Where are my glasses?" I got out and helped Paul search the backseat, floor, and the street. No glasses.

"Oh, here they are," said Renee. The glasses were in her hand where they had been all the time during the search.

As I drove away I couldn't help wondering if Paul really had gotten lucky that night?

I Need to Go Home

One night I had a request from a woman at a local private country club. The club is the oldest and most exclusive in Asheville. It is so particular about its membership and appearance that members or guests are not permitted to park lesser, older, or dirtier cars in the nearest lot in front of the club house. If you don't have a pretty new car and a BMW, Cadillac, or Mercedes, you had better plan to park out-of-sight in the back. I mention this anecdote to help understand the context of this story.

"Maria" was waiting at the front door. She was very young, attractive, and, unexpectedly, pulling a roller suitcase.

"Where do you want to go?" I asked when I saw no destination entered into the app.

"I need to go home," Maria said and she then began to cry.

"I'm sorry, Maria. What's wrong?" I inquired.

"My boyfriend's family hates me! He's such a great guy and I love him so much!" Maria said bawling almost uncontrollably.

"So, how can I help get you home? And where is that?"

"Charlotte. Can you take me to Charlotte? Or maybe just to a hotel? Then I could rent a car tomorrow."

"Since it's 2 in the morning on a weekend, the hotel might not be an option. And you sure can't rent a car until the morning and you'd still need to get to the airport." I gave Maria my advice. I had taken people to Charlotte 100+ miles before. It would cost her about $150. But a hotel and a one way rental car would cost more.

On the way to Charlotte, Maria told her story between a few more bouts of crying:

Maria had graduated from a good southern university in fashion design. Earlier that afternoon, her future Mother-in-Law had said she was not properly dressed for a family picture. She was wearing designer jeans, stylish blouse, high heels and perfect make-up (now tear streaked). She thought she heard her potential Father-in-Law say something that sounded like a racial slur. She thought he said "half-breed." Anyway, they had made it clear that a Latino woman was not suitable for their son. Maria also blubbered that the whole family, except for her almost fiancé, were all "Trump supporters."

Knowing the make-up of that particular country club I was not surprised. We drove on to Charlotte, a two and a half hour ride. I learned that her father was a banker and that they also belonged to a fine country club in Charlotte.

I don't know if Maria ever got back with Charlie or what she did later. On the way to her nice home, she called her mom to tell her what happened.

Her mother was appropriately angry. She told Maria, "Don't you ever let anyone treat you as second-class. You did the right thing. You don't just marry a man; you marry the whole family."

Who Did You Vote For?

On the Saturday night following the 2016 election I picked up a couple of guys, Sam and Ernie, from a downtown bar.

Shortly into the trip Ernie, who was not the paying rider, asked me in a loud drunken slur, "Who did you vote for?"

"Well, Sir, that would be none of your business," I calmly but forcefully replied.

"You look like somebody who voted for that bitch Hilary!" He shouted.

I made no comment, but Sam said, "Shut the fuck up, Ernie!"

But Ernie continued to rant. "I'm gonna punch you (Sam) in the face!"

"OK, that's it." I said pulling over on a dark road by the river. "Get the fuck out of my car!"

"Both of us?" the fare-payer Sam asked.

"No, you're fine, just him."

Ernie got out. Sam said, "Thanks, that asshole can walk home!"

Sam, of course, got a five-star rating for that trip. So did I.

Assault on a Male

I had a pick-up in North Asheville for a young man waiting on the sidewalk. As he got in my car I noticed he had a fat lip and a bloody nose.

"What happened, Tyler?" I asked, offering him a Kleenex.

"My girlfriend hit me in the face." Tyler said.

"Did you hit her back?" I inquired.

"You can't do that. It's assault on a female."

"Yeah, but looks like you were assaulted and battered. You want me to take you to the hospital or police?"

"No. Just take me home."

"Well, how did it happen that she got so mad at you?"

"My girl is a stripper and her girlfriend is a stripper, too. We were drinking

46

and the girls started makin' out. They ended up on the floor naked, doin' their thing, and wanted me to join in with em', but I said I was too drunk and I that I wanted to be going home."

She said, "No you're not!"

I said, "I am calling an Uber and I did. When I got to the door she was screaming at me and then she just hit me in the face!"

"Wow," I said. "That sounds like every man's fantasy turned into a nightmare."

Tyler answered, "I guess so, but all I want to do now is to go home, crawl in bed and try to forget that this night ever happened.

Driving Jesus

One night I had a pick-up at a trailer park in South Asheville. The passenger was Jesus. I correctly pronounced his name 'hey-sus' as the very young Latino man got in my car. He was headed to Waynesville, a town about 35 miles west of Asheville; a longer than usual ride.

I was naturally curious as to why a teenager would have an Uber account as very few do. Usually it's the parent who requests a ride for their kid. He said, "No, it's my Uber account, I have a card."

"That's great!" I said. As a parent I am interested in how today's young people are getting by in this very expensive place to live. "So where do you work?"

"I work for my pops. We paint houses and do drywall. I go to school, too; AB Tech. Construction Technology."

"Beautiful!" I said. The rest of the way we just listened to music. The whole ride to a trailer in Waynesville, that looked much like the one where I picked him up, cost

Jesus about $55.00. He smiled and thanked me for the ride and gave me a $2.00 tip. Most riders tip nothing.

The very next ride was for a very rich woman residing in Biltmore Lakes. The short ride to her multi-million dollar house with a three car garage paid a $5.00 fare with no tip.

She Bit Me!

One night I picked a woman named Ashley, who was going to the Renaissance Hotel, one of Asheville's finest.

I made the usual small talk as a greeting, "How's your day going, Ashley?"

"Well, I hope it gets better!" Ashley replied.

"Oh, what happened?" I asked.

"I got in a fight over there in Aston Park. I kicked some bitch's ass real good! But look what happened to me!"

Ashley was in the front passenger seat. Her very short skirt was already half way up her thighs. Then she pulled her skirt up even higher and said, "Look at this!"

I pulled over and slowed to a near stop. Ashley revealed a saucer sized black, blue, and yellow bruise on her top inner thigh.

"Wow!" I exclaimed, "That looks pretty bad. How did that happen?"

"She bit me! That bitch bit me! Can you believe it?"

"Yeah, I guess I can believe it." I said stretching my imagination a to fill the scene of these girls gone wild fighting

Then Ashley said something I'll not soon forget:

"Do you think I should get a rabies shot?"

"Probably tetanus." I said laughing with her.

Worst Uber Ever

I am proud to say I have done over 13,000 thousand Uber rides and have maintained a 4.9 star rating. The rating system is important for riders as well as drivers. A passenger can view all Driver Profiles to see how their driver stacks up and could cancel a ride if the driver had a low rating.

I know of one driver who gave the rest of Asheville drivers a bad reputation. His car was filthy. He often had his wife in the front seat as he drove her to work and took PAX at the same time. His ratings slipped below 3 stars. Uber sent him a message that his status as an "Uber Partner," as all drivers are called, would end if he did not improve above 4 stars in his next 50 trips. He didn't and he no longer works as an Uber driver.

Some people have reservations about "riding with a stranger" and yet how much would you know about a cab driver?

Probably, they would have no rating system and no driver profile to check-out.

That said, I heard from a woman, Ilsa, a passenger who had a very bad Uber experience: On her Uber trip earlier the same evening, she was riding to her hotel with two other friends; all female. "The ride I had before you was horrible!" Ilsa exclaimed.

"Jeez, what happened?" I asked.

"Our driver went to sleep at the wheel! Can you believe it?"

"No way! That sounds like the most horrible thing I have ever heard in three years of driving for Uber. So, what happened next?"

"I had to shove him to wake him up after he slumped over right here on 240 (the Interstate Expressway). His seatbelt probably kept him from hitting his head on the steering wheel! He woke up and said he was 'so sorry' that he was 'really tired' and that this was his 'last trip of the night'."

"Damn!" I replied. "I hope you gave him a one star (can't give zero) rating and report him to Uber. Anybody who falls asleep driving shouldn't be driving for Uber!"

"I would have," she replied, "But I was so shook up, I forgot. We asked him to pull over and let us out. I told him I didn't want to be in that car for another minute."

"Did he let you out?"

"No! He drove on to our hotel!"

"Good Lord! That amounted to kidnapping!" I exclaimed.

A Scary Ride

One question that riders have asked more than a few times is, "Have you ever had a scary trip or been threatened by a passenger." Well, I haven't, but a fellow driver told me about an incident that had him pretty upset.

One night when the weather was particularly nasty, a driver I know picked up a young guy who seemed unhappy by more than the weather.

The guy mumbled his name in acknowledgement that he was the right passenger and then was silent. He didn't respond to the usual chat about the rain or how his night was going. Just silence.

After about ten minutes of driving, Silent Sam says, "Have you ever wondered what it would feel like to be stabbed?"

The driver, I'll call him Joe, responded after a few seconds to try to imagine why that question was asked, "No I don't think I ever had that thought." Joe was afraid to ask why the passenger asked such a question. He was just relieved to be very near their destination.

The next day he was also happy not to see on TV any news about a stabbing. He still wonders from where that guy got that idea or why he would ask such a question.

The Stench Was Unbearable

The rating system works two ways in that not only do drivers get rated, passengers do as well. I rarely give less than five stars, but in one particular case, the passengers got no more than a three.

I picked up two very attractive young women (based on their faces, figures, and tight leather pants) at a popular bar on North Lexington Street. Both had short blond hair and multiple piercings and tattoos neither of which would be construed as unusual in Asheville.

But the most memorable aspect of the two women was their nearly unbearable body odor. I would not be surprised that they hadn't bathed in a month, if ever. The body odor was so intense I nearly gagged. Now, I have pretty high tolerance for smelly people. Cooks, whom I pick up from various restaurants late after closing, tend to be fairly fragrant. I view that as the smell of a hard-working person and that's not that offensive to me.

These women were way beyond that. It was a warm night, so opening windows on the trip was appropriate. In this case, it was not just appropriate; it seemed a matter of survival! I wanted to say something like "Hey, Iris, have you ever considered bathing?" but just bit my tongue and got them to their place.

I could not pick up other passengers for a while after they had left the car due to the lingering stench. I drove around a bit, windows open to air the car out.

Later, I was taking a bouncer home from another bar. We were chatting about how busy that night had been. I was telling him about the smelly girls.

He said, "Oh, God, they showed up at our place. I got a whiff and wouldn't let them in. The bartender said to me, 'why didn't you let them in? They looked really hot!' I told him why. Jeez, have you ever smelled any humans with more B.O. than that?"

"No!" I replied. "That would be a record for me."

Feeling Really Old

One night around 2:30 AM I was waiting a long time; in Uber time that's more than five minutes for the woman to appear who had requested the ride. Marlene finally came out, got in the car, but wanted me to wait for two other riders. She said, "I'm sorry to make you wait. I'm really feeling old. Younger people just have any respect for others."

"So what's happening?" I asked.

"There's this 42 year old guy hitting on a 30 year old woman. I told them Uber was here, but they just keep talking."

"Friends of yours?"

"Well, sort of. The 42 year old guy is Dave, my husband. He says he is interviewing a Mexican girl for a job."

Finally, Dave appears smoking a cigarette with a latina woman, the 30 year old. He asks if he can smoke in my car. I say "Not in my car."

Marlene, snaps at Dave, "You know you can't smoke in an Uber!" Dave puts the smoke out and gets in the back seat with Carmen.

He says, "Can we take this girl home? She lives on the way to our house."

"No problem." I replied.

"We'll pay you extra." Dave said.

"That's OK, if it's on the way, no extra charge."

Dave and Carmen continue the conversation about the job, not what it is, but how much Dave is willing to pay. Seems to be a rather large gap between what Carmen says she is worth and what Dave says he can pay.

We arrived at the top of a dirt road off of a main road behind a pizza restaurant. Carmen says, "I can get out here."

I said, "I don't mind taking you down there." The dirt road was dark without any street lights.

Dave says, "She'll be ok." So Carmen got out and started walking.

Marlene, sitting in the front seat says, "It's dark down there. Walter said he's fine with driving her to her house."

"She'll be fine walking. She's a Mexican."

Marlene said, "You are an asshole, Dave!"

Things were quiet the last three miles to Marlene and Dave's house.

When we arrived at their driveway, Dave got out before Marlene. She handed me a twenty dollar tip. Dave was going for his wallet, but Marlene stopped him. "I gave him a tip." She said.

"How much?" Said Dave.

"Two dollars." Marlene lied. Then she leaned toward me and said, "I'd like to see you again real soon."

Employee's Only

I took four women back from town to the campground where they said ten of their friends were staying in a cabin. On the way one exclaimed, "Hey, there's our gas station!"

She explained they had been picked up earlier that night by a female Uber driver who, shortly after they were on the trip to town, cut a loud fart that required the lowering of all windows. "Oh I am so sorry." The driver apologized. "I'm going to have to stop at this gas station to use the restroom."

"That's OK, Honey." The PAX said. "We understand."

A minute later the Uber driver appeared very distressed saying, "The guy at the cash register won't let me use the bathroom! He said it's for EMPLOYEES ONLY!" The Uber driver then messed her pants. All the riders got out as the diver said she was very embarrassed but could not continue the trip. She told them they would have to get another Uber.

As the driver left, the passengers went into the station and gave the clerk a loud piece of their minds. He said he didn't make the rules. Another Uber arrived in a few minutes to get the group to town.

A Good Place to Go

I am often asked where the best places to go in Asheville for food, drink, and fun. I am never asked one of the most important questions faced daily by Uber drivers: Where are the restrooms? A couple of years ago the Republican Majority North Carolina Legislature had passed a law that required people to use the appropriately designated male or female restroom that corresponded to the gender of one's birth. The unintended consequence of that inane law was losing a great deal of corporate investment in the state; major sports tournaments pulling out of venues in the state; and mainly making a great state the butt of many jokes.

"Do I need a Birth Certificate to use a restroom?" Someone from Michigan asked me, laughing.

The so-called 'Bathroom Bill' was later changed, but was a contributing factor in Governor Pat McCrory losing his job to a Democrat in a state that went for Trump. Most restrooms in Asheville are now designated bi-gender, so now you can go anywhere, except those that are posted 'Employees Only'.

The dilemma for Uber drivers is the length of time behind the wheel and the steady stream of ride requests. Pit stops become an issue.

My personal favorite restrooms are #1 The Omni Grove Park Inn; nicely appointed with plenty of paper, private stalls, and excellent décor. #2 The Renaissance Hotel which also is spotlessly clean, newly renovated, and warm and well stocked with paper products. #3 The Doubletree Hotel where you can find a great cup of coffee for $2.00 and a free hot chocolate chip cookie to follow your excellent toilet experience. And #4 would have to be The Hilton Garden Inn on College Street featuring amazing ultra modern design and a futuristic sink.

Heather by the Dumpster

One night I went to pick up a young woman at the Grey Eagle, one of the many popular music venues in Asheville. As I approached, "Heather" called me. Contacting a driver is one of the many aspects of using the ride share service that makes it far better than a taxi.

Heather said, "This is Heather." She was speaking in a low voice. "Please drive past the Grey Eagle and pick me up down by the dumpster."

"Ok, yes I see it. Where are you?"

"I'm behind the dumpster."

I pulled into the vacant lot beside a dumpster and Heather appeared and quickly got into the car crouching down below the passenger window.

"What's up, Heather? Are you OK?"

"Yes. Three of my ex-boyfriends all showed up there tonight. I don't want to

talk with any of them. It's just really weird and
awkward."

As we drove back past the Grey
Eagle, Heather was invisible and, I suppose,
the three guys standing there were wondering
how Heather had disappeared so quickly.

Homeless Girl

Late one night another driver friend of mine said he picked up a young woman who was crying. She said her boyfriend just kicked her out of his apartment. She said she had no place to go.

My friend could not think what to do, so he called me for advice. I said, "Since the homeless shelter is closed for the night, I really don't know what you can do for her. Maybe get her a room? The fact that she has a credit card means she has some money, right?"

Later he told me she said she didn't have enough money for a hotel. The driver then had a brilliant idea: call the boyfriend back and plead with him to stay one more night. It worked!

The homeless girl had at least one more night and the rest of her life to deal with boyfriend and homelessness.

A Celebrity Ex

A passenger related the story of a recent Uber ride she had had while on vacation in Utah. I think she said in Park City.

She said, "I always ask the driver what they like about driving for Uber and maybe something about their life."

"So, this guy, Richard, says he liked driving and didn't really need the money. He said he once had a restaurant in Beverly Hills and met lots of movie star celebrities there. One night, he said he met his future wife there"

"Oh, who was that?" she asked.

"Raquel Welch! Would you believe it?"

"No! I don't believe it!"

"Well, Google 'Raquel Welch's husbands.' There I am, Richard Palmer, #4."

He was right, Richard Palmer, Celebrity Ex and Uber Driver!

He Sold Me a Book

One recent night I picked up four guys from Charlotte. One of them had been in Asheville last year. "Bill" told the story of an Uber driver who was also a writer.

"Last time I was here, I asked the driver what he did besides driving for Uber. The driver said he was also a writer. I asked him what he wrote and he said "lots of things." He said he wrote a sci-fi novel last year. He told me about it and said I could buy it from the trunk of his car. I did."

At that point I was about to crack-up having to stifle a laugh because the Uber Driver/Writer was me! The buyer of my novel, *Morph: The Resurrection of Angels* didn't recognize me and I did not confess. I should have asked how he liked it, but refrained.

That was one of about 375 copies I have sold to people who asked what I did besides Ubering.

In case you might be interested, *Morph:the Resurrection of Angels* is available from Amazon as a Kindle as well as in paperback. It is a tale based on the premise that angels might have been real; a higher form of humanity that metamorphosed when the age of 125 years was attained. Nobody has lived that long in thousands of years due to war, disease, malnourishment, etc.

Curiously, nearly every mythology and religion around the world has flying people among their ancient beliefs. Universally these beings do the same thing: they deliver messages to people; presumably from God or the gods. They carry messages of wisdom that the higher power wants them to know. Also, interestingly, our word 'angel' comes from the ancient Greek word *angelos* which means, literally, 'messenger'.

The novel begins in Amiens, France, in 1948. There, amidst the rubble of the bombed out railway station, a prehistoric barrow has been discovered. A team of archeologists, Americans, Professor Arthur Barringer and his assistant Myra Rosenblum, are brought in from Oxford University by the Louvre Museum to investigate. The team finds the expected crypt and, inside the coffin, the mummified remains of a king. So they think.

Two things were immediately surprising: One was the size of the mummy, about 6'5". And, unexpectedly, a pair of very large wings had been placed on either side of the body. They had not seen anything like that before. Barrows, small burial mounds, dot the landscape all over northern Europe. I have been in several of them myself.

However, the real shock to the archeologist and his assistant came when they turned the mummy over. There were huge scapulae protruding through the grayish skin of the back. It appeared that something had been hacked or sawn off these backbones. Then they made the astounding observation that the bottom of the wings in coffin had matching marks to the scapulae. The wings had been removed from the corpse! Barringer and Rosenblum had found an angel!

That would have been the greatest discovery of the 20th Century, if not all time, but there was a problem: The professor and archeologist had been one of the skeptics of the so-called Piltdown Man (see Wikipedia). That discovery in 1912 by an amateur archeologist named Dawson had been hailed by leading scientists of that time as the long sought "Missing Link." Any scientists who would question Piltdown as a fraud, were not allowed to examine the skull. It remained hallowed in a glass case in the British Museum for forty years.

So, the chief skeptic of Piltdown has a real dilemma. Professor Arthur Barringer can't say, "Piltdown man is a fake, but, by the way, last week my assistant Myra and I have found an angel!" He would be laughed out of the academy. So Barringer and his graduate assistant make a pact that they will not reveal what they found until they can prove that the angel is real or an elaborate fake.

That's a synopsis of Chapter 1 of a 40 chapter book. To read further, buy *Morph* at an Asheville bookstore, on line at Amazon.com, or, if you are really lucky, out of the trunk of my car!

The Knuckle Cracker

I picked up "Aden" from a downtown bar to take him to a West Asheville bar that was featuring a burlesque show that night.

Aden stared straight ahead; not talking or smiling, but shortly into the trip he cracked his knuckles. Some people may find that habit irritating. I don't because I do that myself.

My Grandma once told me to stop doing that saying, "That's going to make your knuckles big and ugly and stiff like Aunt Nellie" Aunt Nell was her oldest sister and in her late eighties at the time.

Before I could relay that warning to Aden, he volunteered, "They used to say knuckle cracking was bad for you, but now they say it helps make your fingers more flexible."

"Really?" I replied, "What makes that noise?"

"It's a combination of cartilage and the release of nitrogen gas."

"Where does the gas go?" I asked.

"I don't know; probably just a tiny bit. I am a musician and it helps my fingers move fast."

"What do you play, Aden?"

"Guitar and piano; mostly classical."

Aden asked if I played an instrument. "No, but I appreciate all kinds of music." I am a writer.

"Oh, I do that too."

"What do you write?"

"Poetry, short stories, and I am working on a novel. I can type faster than I can talk and I don't have to revise much. I can type 160 words-per-minute with few errors. What do you write?"

"Well, I have published a couple of books and I'm working on another one now. I never really learned to type so I use three fingers and knuckle cracking hasn't helped my speed which is probably less than 40 wpm."

Aden was curious about my novel and at the end of the trip he bought one.

Get out of My Car!

Most Uber drivers, if they drive enough passengers on enough trips, will have incidents they wish they could have avoided. Such was the case of the driver who had a passenger who refusing to leave the car when they arrived at the designated drop-off address.

The woman did not believe that the driver had taken her to the right place. She said over and over, "This is not my destination. Take me to my destination."

The driver insisted that he had arrived at the place shown in the app. He showed her the app pinpointing their location as the correct spot for the drop-off. "Now, get out of my car!"

She continued to refuse and in a very calm voice continued to say she was not where she wanted to go. All the while she recorded the incident on her phone. The whole episode lasts about three minutes in which the driver becomes more and more upset and profane in his response to her refusal. You really should see this:

Youtube.com/watch?v=HmJy1FRRHis which has been viewed millions of times and even turned into a cartoon video.

My own take on this, or shall we say, what I would have done: More calmly go around and open the door. Show her once again that she was where she wanted to be according to the app. As it turned out, the driver had taken her to the designated medical facility, but not on the side of the building she expected to be. Someone at the clinic escorted her through the building to the spot not on the driver's GPS.

This was a case of two immovable objects colliding... a rare phenomenon in physics, but maybe not in Uber world.

Uber Scandals

Uber has had more than a few scandals that range anywhere from hiding vast amounts of money offshore; to sexual harassment of employees; to stealing technical information on autonomous vehicles from a rival company. Perhaps one of the least scandalous was also the most visible and notorious.

That was when Travis Kalanick, the controversial CEO and founder of Uber was recorded berating an Uber driver in New York City in response to a driver complaining to him about the drastic reduction in fare prices in that city. See it on YouTube.

It is hard to say which scandal resulted in the most losses to Uber either lost ridership or through being on the losing side of multiple lawsuits that cost the company hundreds of millions of dollars.

I am mentioning this because I myself have been affected by the national scandals. People who used to use Uber now use Lyft. I had to also sign up with Lyft to avoid the drop in ridership. Still Uber is by far the most used ride share app in Asheville and I still derive more income from it than its competitor.

People often ask "What's better, Uber or Lyft?"

I point out that Lyft had a couple of advantages that Uber did not have such as tipping via the credit card on the app and the convenience of adding multiple stops to a trip. Uber fixed that and now they are identical in those regards. Lyft has much quicker personal support for drivers than Uber. I attribute that to size of the company. More about Lyft vs Uber later in this book.

Uber Clean-up Scam and Not

A driver's worst night mare is people getting sick and vomiting in their car. In all my 13,000 Uber rides and 3,000 more with Lyft, that has happened only once. I was paid the $150 fee that is charged by Uber to the puker and passed on to me, the pukee. Trust me, that $150 is not enough especially when a driver may lose two nights of income before the car smells good enough again to have passengers.

I think this story comes from Miami: Apparently some driver (or drivers) in that city was claiming the Vomit Fee when no such thing happened. They took required photos of the mess (faked) and submitted It seems that fraud would be easy to detect based on some statistical average? I mean, three a week? Come on!

Anyway, my experience of having only one case of spew in my car may be better than most drivers. That said, I have become keenly aware of the propensity of a passenger to go from a quietly drunken man or woman to one on the verge of vomiting.

One night I picked up three guys from a bar. One of them could barely walk. The other two were relatively sober and fully aware that their friend, Bill, was either comatose or about to upchuck. They kept talking to him like you see somebody trying to keep a dying person alive, "Stay with me Bill! Hold my hand! Squeeze my hand. We are almost there!"

The sober ones kept apologizing to me. "We are so sorry about this. It's Bill's birthday and he has probably had too many shots and beers." Probably? No kidding!

I told them to give Bill a sick sack; a repurposed plastic grocery bag that I keep in a pouch behind the front seat. They gave him the bag. I also told them, "Let me know if they think vomiting was inevitable. I will pull over."

Soon they exclaimed, "Pull over! He's about to puke. I did. They got him out in a brightly lit convenience store parking lot. I don't think I have seen anyone blow chunks more forcefully than Bill did. It was volcanic. Mt Vesuvius!

We were very close to the drop-off. When we arrived about two minutes later the Bill's friend gave me another apology and two twenty dollar bills.

A Treasure Club Patron

Several times a week I take guys, and a few women, to the Treasure Club. I also give dancers rides to and from there. I get asked frequently if the Treasure Club is the best strip club in Asheville. "Yes it is. It is the only strip club in Asheville," I reply.

One night, a short, bespectacled, balding man in his 50's got in my car. Ralph was going to Black Mountain about 15 miles east.

Ralph said, "I don't think my church knows that I drink. And they sure wouldn't want me going to no strip joint."

Ralph said he was not a religious person, but he worked at a Christian Ministry in Black Mountain. Ralph asked the same question I get from many riders, "Is Uber your full time job?

"No. I'm a writer. I write books." Then I go on to tell about my novel, *Morph: the Resurrection of Angels* and *Uber & Out.* Ralph repeated his earlier statement that he was not religious. I assured him that *Morph* was not a religious book. "It is science fiction."

Ralph asked it was a Kindle. I said it was. Ralph downloaded a copy before we got to his home.

Becoming an Uber Driver

One question I get, not infrequently, is "I was thinking about doing Uber myself. How does that work?"

I am more than happy to tell them, since, of course, I get a referral incentive. The new driver also gets a bonus in a guarantee of at least $200 for doing their first 30 rides. Looking at my own 30 ride average; that amounts to $50-75 more than the fares alone would pay.

If you, reading this, want to be an Uber driver, here's what you need: Go to the driver app on Google Play™ or the Apple Store™ and follow the instructions. Using my referral code WKFP6 you'll get the bonus mentioned above. Here are the requirements:

- A car that is no more than 15 years old and inspected. It must have 4 doors and accommodate 4 passengers. A regular sedan or compact SUV is called an "UberX" and qualifies for standard fares. A large 5-9 passenger SUV can be an "UberXL" which pays more per mile and time than an X.

- A clean driving record; that is no serious traffic offences for 5 years.
- Automobile insurance. You must have regular auto insurance even though when you are on Uber business you are under the umbrella of Uber's own insurance policy. Some insurance companies will refuse to insure anyone driving for Uber. I find that odd, since they would have no liability if an accident occurred as you were driving for

Uber. Uber covers that eventuality. You must submit a copy of your insurance card showing that it is up-to-date.

- The car must be registered in your name. You will need to provide a copy of that card.
- Pictures of yourself, The documents must be current and the picture of the driver is used for random, monthly selfies that keep that image current as well as matching with facial recognition in the account.

Uber conducts a background check through their partners Checkr and Raiser, Inc. Raiser is also the payroll department of Uber.

Once you apply for Uber, it takes 4-5 business days for processing the background check and documents.

After that brief wait of a few days, you should be good to go. Uber does not provide a tutorial on how to use the driver app, but it is very intuitive. You click the app icon and a screen appears with a local map. You go on-line by touching the button that says off-line and then you are on-line. You will get a "ping" that is a ride request showing where to go to pick someone up. You touch the pulsating and chiming logo on the map screen. You then have the name of the pax and their pick-up point.

That, by the way, is one of the two main reasons Uber is safe transportation. The other reason is that your passenger has your "profile" including your name and a little information about you. And you can call or text each other. Compare that to riding, or driving, a taxi!

Recently North Carolina passed a law in response to a tragic incident in Columbia, South Carolina: A young woman student at USC was murdered by a man who let her into his car. It was not an Uber. Just a random car that accepted her error in thinking it was her ride.

The new law requires an Uber or Lyft car to post their license plate number on the lower right of the windshield. This is in addition to that number and other driver information on the rider's app. The new law goes into effect January 1, 202o

Uber vs. Lyft

My passengers often ask which ride-sharing platform I like best. The simple answer is, "I don't really have a preference since they are nearly identical. I just accept the ride request that comes up first, then immediately turn the other app off."

Nationwide, Uber is more popular than Lyft, but in some cities Lyft has overtaken Uber. The many scandals have given Uber enough bad press to cause people to switch to Lyft or another ride-share platform. In Asheville there are only three choices for ride-sharing. At this time Uber rides are 3-4 times more popular than Lyft.

A third company is the locally owned Asheville Ride which allows people to drive their one vehicle or one from their own fleet. The rides they do are dispatched like taxis. Typical rides cost more than Uber or Lyft and the drivers are paid a bit more if drivers use their own cars.

There are many similarities and some differences in the national ride-share services. Both Uber and Lyft pay about the same. They use different formulas to calculate how much they pay drivers. On a minimum fare ride, as of this writing, Uber is paying me $3.20; Lyft pays $3.00. But on a hypothetical 10 mile trip lasting 15 minutes, Lyft pays me $8.80 and Uber $8.00. This is assuming no "surge" (high demand time) pricing. Lyft calls a surge "Prime Time." Uber's algorithm for a surge is more precise down do areas of half a block increments and 10ths of a percent in the fare increase. Lyft uses rectangles for fare increase that seem even more arbitrary than Uber's.

Lyft also has a gimmick to keep drivers in their platform: they show bonus increments of 3 cents every five seconds up to a maximum of around $5.00/ride. The clock runs during wait time in Prime Time zones.

Nearly all of my passengers who regularly use Uber have their own horror stories of being charged big surge fees at some time, especially around New Years. Savvy riders know if they just wait a while, often just a few minutes, the surge will subside completely or go down several levels.

I know Uber and Lyft have studied the surge as a business decision, but from a PR standpoint, it seems like they could do better. For example, they could have a flat rate increase, say, five or ten dollars for nights, holidays, weekends, or whatever they decide.

That way there would be no surprises. Both Uber and Lyft still would be way less than taxi fares and the riders, I believe, would have far fewer complaints.

When Lyft started, nationally about a year after Uber, they offered the ability to use the credit card on the account to leave a tip for drivers. It took several years for Uber to offer the same feature. Still, Lyft riders seem more likely than Uber riders to tip on the card.

Another feature that Lyft has that was not, until recently, was the ability of a rider to enter multiple stops and round trips in the app. Uber fixed that also following Lyft's lead.

One advantage that Uber had over Lyft was getting a request for another ride while on a ride. The next trip usually begins near the drop-off of the first ride so that is a very efficient feature. Lyft started the same feature with the announcement: "A new ride has been added to your queue."

Both Lyft and Uber make direct deposits to my checking account every week on Tuesday or Wednesday around 2:00 AM. The pay calculations are accurate down to the 10th of a mile and second in drive time. The pay week runs from 3:00 AM EST Monday to 2:59 EST next Monday.

              The only other advantage that Lyft has over Uber is that of customer and driver support. With Uber it is very difficult to actually speak with a customer support person. Like so many other so-called support platforms, there are canned responses that usually don't apply to the question at hand. You must leave email messages and get responses that are often off the mark. With Lyft, one simply requests a call back at the number you have in their database. They call back in less than a minute and a real person addresses the issue you may have and resolves the problem immediately. I think this is really great and remarkable in a day when the norm is "your call is very important to us" followed by a long wait on hold or the invitation to visit a convoluted website.

Uber and Lyft at the AVL Airport

One afternoon, sort of out of the blue, I received an email from Uber saying we were no longer allowed to pick up passengers at the Asheville airport. I was dumbstruck. "What the hell happened?" I thought.

Turns out that Asheville Airport Authority had arbitrarily decided to charge Uber a fee per ride to pick people up. Until Uber figured out exactly where the fee would come from, they summarily stopped serving arriving passengers by blocking the app at the airport. We were still permitted by Uber and the airport to drop people off at the terminal, but then had to leave to work elsewhere.

The Airport claims that a fee in commonplace at other airports and that they just followed suit. Of course, the real reason is just another way for somebody or some organization to make more money. It took two months for Uber (and Lyft) figure out how to collect the fee from their clients and pass the money on to the Airport Authority. The fee is now invisibly collected and paid as a pass-through cost.

The night the new policy was in effect, I picked up a young guy with a roller bag at McDonald's, a quarter mile from the terminal. It was raining. He had first walked across the highway to a hotel. The Fairfield Inn was apparently too close to the terminal and was in the prohibited area. Then he kept walking up a main road with no sidewalk, across an Interstate Highway interchange, and on. He checked to see if he could make an Uber request and was not successful until he had come to McDonald's.

I told the wet passenger that this whole thing was outrageous. I later learned, in the local newspaper the next day, that the Airport Authority had informed Uber about their plans to charge a fee some three months before, but Uber made no mention of this to their drivers until the day the policy took effect.

Uber had been paying the Asheville Airport Authority $7,000 for the privilege of using the cell phone lot at the airport to stage the driver queue to pick up passengers. Apparently the AVL wanted more.

Local taxi companies already pay a fee so they were not affected. Now, if Uber charged as much as taxis, they could certainly afford the fee as well. Currently, it costs passengers roughly 50% more to take a taxi from the airport to Downtown Asheville as that same trip costs with Uber. There is no doubt that the fee will be passed through. And there is no doubt that drivers will not get any more pay for trips from the airport due to a fee collection.

The issue was finally resolved, although the flying public is still inconvenienced by having to walk farther to a side lot that splits off of the main terminal drive. There is no shelter there in case of rain and since nothing is done about that this is a real problem especially in the winter.

Fired by Uber and Lyft

I mentioned that Uber (and Lyft as well) will fire you for low ratings. As I learned personally, they will fire you anyway despite your near perfect record, long service, and very high ratings.

Here's what happened to me: One night, a woman backed into my car on a downtown street. The damage was minor, but these days a fender bender can cost more the $500. I was not in my car at the time and not of Uber business. I called police because I did not want to use a $500 deductable to pay for repairs. Her insurance did pay so that was done.

Two years later, in January 2018, I was driving on a major five-lane thoroughfare with three Uber passengers. From a parking lot on the opposite side of the road a young man with two female passengers came at high speed directly across the road and totaled his car and mine. Three cops, two ambulances, and a fire truck came. Fortunately all of us were buckled up and the air bags went off. Nobody in my car was hurt.

Uber's insurance company verified from a police report that the accident had not been my fault and that Uber had no liability. The other driver's insurance paid for a new car for me and even compensated me for lost wages.

Eleven months later, Uber got its annual background check from a company called Checkr. They said because my DMV report showed two accidents, my account was "deactivated" (i.e. fired). I learned that the DMV reports accidents without showing who was at fault. It turned out that Uber does not care if a driver was at fault or not. Guess it is just too much trouble or they just don't care. A month after that, Lyft, also using an automated background check, fired me as well.

In April, another background check showed that I had only one accident (that old fender bender dropped off the DMV record) and my accounts were restored.

Uber and Lyft Drivers As Employees?

       Effective January 1, 2020, California's "B5" law takes effect. This law changes the status of drivers Uber, Lyft, and many other independent contractors including food delivery services. As employees these workers would now get minimum wages, benefits, etc.

       There are many problems with this law. Uber, Lyft, Doordash and others are spending millions to get the law changed in a referendum in the fall of 2020.

       While I am sympathetic to anyone who has to do these "gigs" to make a living, rather than supplement their income, someone like me has more to lose than gain by employee designation.
       First of all, independent contractors chose to work when, where and if they even want to. We have no direct supervisor; no shift set; no required days on or off. As to minimum wage? I don't' work unless I am making $20/hr gross. Yes, I do have to pay for all expenses on my car, but that's counted by the IRS as income reduction for taxes at the rate of fifty-five cents per mile.

Being old, I am on
Medicare, so health benefits as an employee
are unlikely to be better than what I have now.

I have heard that a $30/hr
minimum wage is being suggested for gig
workers. Fat chance of that happening! Be
that as it may, there is absolutely no way an
employer such as Uber could allow its
employees to work when an if they so choose.
Rather they would have minimum hours and
those scheduled at peak times as demand for
the service dictates.

The Gig Economy is all about
independence both for the workers who supply
the rides and food delivery and their clients
who demand those services. Uber is shown to
have greatly expanded transportation options.

No longer do people have to live
near bus or train lines to get to work or near
shopping and entertainment. They don't have
to pay the relatively high cost of taxi service for
transportation needs.

I predict the people of California
will defeat the onerous B5 law in the next
election.

She Cheated on Me

One night I was Downtown when a request came in from Leicester, about fifteen miles north of Asheville. If the trip been back to town, the long pick-up drive there would have been worth the drive. That was not the case.

When I got to the small white frame house very near Newfound Road, the passenger was nowhere to be seen. I waited several minutes then called. "I'm out front. Are you coming?

There was no reply. I was about call it a "no show" and pull away when a man appeared on the porch. There was some yelling and he went back in the house for many minutes. Again, I was just about to leave when he appeared and walked to the car carrying a large bag.

He got in and appeared to be very upset. "I just caught my wife cheatin' on me!"

"I'm sorry," I said. "So you want to go into Asheville?"

"No. Just take me up to the store."

"You mean the store right up there?" I said pointing to a convenience store which was within easy walking distance even with a large bag. I was irritated for several reasons: the long drive from town; the long wait for him to get in the car; and, now, the minimum fare ride, $3.20 to me.

"Yeah, I just need to get out of that house!"

I dropped the man off less than 200 yards away. I was pretty pissed off even though I was sympathetic to his plight. When he gave me a $20 tip, all was well. 5 stars!

Another Dubious 5 Star PAX

The last story reminded me of another time I was really irritated with riders. I had waited nearly 20 minutes for this "party" to get in the car. They kept going back to the party house, coming out, going back, yelling and laughing all the while I was waiting. I must not have paid good enough attention to the fact that I had one passenger, the payee, up front and four of his loud and obnoxious friends in the three passenger back seat. That's illegal in NC, but I was already on my way before I noticed.

On the way the PAX explained that he was the sales manager of a car dealership and the people in the back, one woman and the others, male, were his salespeople. They were as loud as you can imagine drunken "Type A" people to be. All talked over one another with voices that could be heard a block away not just inches from my ears and those of everyone else in the car.

As they got out at the designated destination, my finger was poised above the app to rate them two stars or less. Then the manager slipped me a twenty dollar bill. Now that's what I call a 5 Star passenger!

Wet Dog on the Loose

Most of the stories related in *Uber & Out* are not only true, but are told as observations of other people, my passengers, or PAX of other drivers. This one was all of my own misunderstanding, or, I confess, my own good intentions however stupid.

A week before this event, my son's roommate's dog, a pit bull mix named "Winnie" had escaped the yard and had run off down a very busy road in Asheville. Frantically the boys searched and, ultimately, found her a quarter of a mile away.

That was on my mind when I picked a man up on a side street about a block from my son's place and saw a large brown dog running loose. I was sure that was "Winnie" run off again.

I said to my passenger, "Oh, gosh, I think that dog belongs to my son's roommate. Do you mind if I get her back to her home? It's just a block away."

The guy said, "No problem. That's good."

It was cold and raining when I called, "Here, Winnie! That's a good girl." And she came running to me out of the darkness; her tail wagging. "Get in the car," I ordered and she climbed obediently into the back seat.

We drove the three blocks to my son's house. I stopped in the driveway and I opened the door and the dog got out and followed me to the porch

A couple of seconds later my son opened the door even though it was 1:00 AM. As he opened the door, Winnie went running into his house.

"I found her nearby running loose," I explained.

My son exclaimed, "That's not Winnie! She's in the backroom asleep!"

"Oh, shit!" I replied. Now that I see her in the light, I can see she's the wrong dog!"

We let her out and I went on with the Uber ride, embarrassed and apologetic. The passenger was not laughing.

The Skinwalker

One night I picked up a young man at McDonald's near Asheville Airport. I learned that Jason needed a ride to Jupiter, NC. That is thirty miles from the pick-up. On longer rides I usually hear much of the life story of the passenger. That was the case with Jason.

First Jason said, "I've worked sixty hours this week."

"Wow," I said, "You must be really tired.

"I'm not tired. I just hate to sleep. I have been up a hundred and forty-seven straight hours."

"You're kidding, right?" I asked incredulously.

"Nope. And this is not the longest I have gone without sleeping. I just hate to sleep. I've always been like this."

I tried to discern some signs of, perhaps, drug abuse, but Jason seemed perfectly normal and coherent. "I guess that can't be called insomnia because that's when you want to sleep, but can't."

"That's right. I'm okay. They say I shouldn't be. I am a Cherokee. My grandma is full blooded; my mom is half."

Note that the Eastern Band of the Cherokee Nation is located in Western, North Carolina and there are many Cherokee throughout this part of the state.

Jason went on to say that his Grandma told him he was descended from Skinwalkers. I confessed not knowing what that was.

Jason explained, "When a man kills an animal, he can take the skin or hide from that animal. He puts that skin on and becomes that animal. He takes on the soul of that animal."

I asked him, "Do you know what animal you might be descended from."

"I like night better than day. So maybe a cat or a bat."

"Well," I said, "Cats sleep a lot and bats sleep in caves."

Jason agreed, "I don't know of any animals that don't sleep. Just me."

Channeling Janis Joplin

Late one night, after a long trip to the far side of Weaverville, some twenty miles north of Asheville (the Skin Walker ride) I thought I would have an empty trip back to town. I was lucky in that the next pick-up was nearby at The Thunderbird Tavern less than ten miles from the Tennessee state line.

A highly intoxicated young woman, resembling the late Janis Joplin was the passenger. She needed a ride home farther north and west and even closer to the Tennessee line. As with other long rides, you hear a lot of a person's life story.

Janis, as I will call her, said, "I'm glad to get out of there."

"What happened?" I asked.

"My family goes back nine generations in these mountains. We are proud of that. This dude started running his mouth about my daddy. Nobody talks that way about Daddy! If I'd had a gun I would have shot him."

"Did you get into a fight?"

"Damn right I did! Broke a beer bottle and was goin' at him. They stopped me so nobody got hurt.   They had a karaoke going and they asked me to sing *Me and My Bobby McGee.*"

"You know that's really funny," I replied. "When I first saw you I was thinking you looked kind of like Janis Joplin."

She laughed at that and said "I get that all the time." Then she began singing "Oh Lord won't you buy be a Mercedes Benz/ My friends all drive Porches, I must make amends."

I joined in with the rest of the song. When we got to her place way up on a mountainside she invited me in to smoke a joint. I declined. It was 2:30 AM and I had to get back to Asheville.

A Side Piece

A female Uber driver told me this story: One night she had a call from an upscale suburban neighborhood. It was from a man named "Bob".

As she waited in the driveway behind a big BMW which was facing out, she rolled down the windows. It was a warm Friday summer night. She was waiting up to the limit almost to the "no show" time. But she continued waiting because she heard what sounded like a heated argument coming from inside.

Then a woman appeared carrying a bag and wearing nothing but a white bathrobe with the name "Bob" embroidered on it. The woman's streaming red hair was wet.

"Where's Bob?" the driver asked.

"The son-of-a-bitch isn't coming! He got this ride for me. I'm his Side Piece. His old lady is on her way. Came back a day early wouldn't ya know. So he pulls me out of the shower and called an Uber."

The woman then began dressing herself in the back seat. When that was hurriedly done, she said to the driver,

"Hey, I forgot something. Can you take me back there?"

"Sounds kinda dangerous," the driver replied.

"It'll be okay, she's coming from the airport in an Uber."

The driver went on, "We got back to Bob's house and she got out and ran up the driveway. She picked up a rock and smashed the windshield of the BMW. Then she got back in the car. I saw Bob on the front steps yelling something as I made the get-away. I'm thinking, was I an accessory to a crime? What if I get pulled over? Thank God we didn't."

She took Side Piece to her downtown hotel thinking that Bob would be unlikely to report the vandalism though having much to explain to his wife.

The Hippie Bus

One night last May I picked up a young couple, Travis and Brianna, celebrating their first year of marital bliss. They were from Michigan but had been married in Asheville. On the way down from Kalamazoo, they had seen the Kentucky Derby which had been on their bucket list a long time.

Brianna said she had found a "perfect Asheville AirBnB" for them. It was actually a converted school bus from the 1960's adorned with flowers and peace signs. It was hollowed out on the inside, as she described it, to accommodate a bed, small fridge, microwave, a small table and a couple of chairs. It did not have running water, however, and Brianna said, "This is the first time in my life using an outhouse!"

The "hippie bus" was located in Weaverville about fifteen miles north of downtown Asheville. On rides of that length, it often comes up that in addition to Ubering, I also am a writer.

"Oh, what do you write?" the PAX asks.

"Books," I reply and then my usual answer to "What kind of books?" leads to the narrative described earlier regarding *Morph: the Resurrection of Angels* and then to my closing line, "As a matter of fact, you can buy one from the trunk of my car."

"Really?" Travis asked, "How much?"

"Ten dollars. Or at Amazon for $12.95."

The couple had been discussing a bottle of fine wine they had purchased as part of this anniversary honeymoon. Travis said, "I hope the bus has a corkscrew."

Travis said he'd buy a book if I had change for a twenty. I said, "I don't think I have change, but I do have a corkscrew!" I had an all-purpose Swiss Army Knife knock-off in the console of my car.

When we arrived at the hippie bus, I autographed a copy of *Morph,* and, for twenty dollars, sold them a book and a corkscrew. They laughed and said the ride was their best Uber ride ever.

Possible Swingers

Occasionally while driving I pick up on an uncomfortable conversation. Such was the case one night when I picked up Andrea and her husband Jason at a popular bar on the South Slope, the area of Asheville that has several bars and ten breweries.

As they got in the car, Andrea said to Jason, "I just don't understand why you left with her."

"Sheila asked me to go with her to get cigarettes."

"Well, you don't smoke and you know I hate smoking! And you left me talking to Eric, her husband." Andrea said, getting increasing agitated.

"Baby, it was nothing, I swear. What did Eric have to say?"

"Jason, I think he was trying to pick me up!"

Jason replied, "Yeah, I think they are swingers. I asked why she didn't get Eric to take her to get her smokes. She said, 'don't worry about him...he's a big boy and can take of himself.'"

The rest of the trip was marked chilly silence with only my Pandora radio station playing distantly in the background.

As I pulled in their driveway, Jason was still trying to make up to Andrea. "I swear to God, Baby, nothing happened!"

Andrea's lack of response spoke volumes.

Ten Thousand Rides

On March 14, 2017, I reached a personal milestone: My 10,000th Uber ride. I was alerted to this fact by a couple who had noticed the ride count on my Uber profile on the app. (Update: Now I'm close to 13,000 on Uber and have nearly 4,000 on Lyft.)

"Pull over!" the woman said. We just saw that we are your 9,999th ride. "Can we stop, end that trip, and get you again so we will be ten thousandth?"

Her boyfriend vetoed the idea saying "We'll be just as happy knowing we are part of your driving history, the 9,999 th."

My next passengers were also impressed. They wanted me to blow my horn all the way through Beaucatcher Mountain Tunnel. I gave them a couple of sustained toots.

Uber has yet to acknowledge my achievement. Some time ago, I received a personal text message from Uber saying, "Congratulations, Walter. You have done 5,000 rides with Uber." I know that text was especially personal only to me because it had my name included. I'm sure someone high up at Uber wrote that. Right? Uh, no!

A little while later I received, in the mail, a special sticker for my windshield: UBER VIP it reads. There was no explanation as to what VIP means. I think I got a bonus of one dollar for each ride for a week. Perhaps a couple of shares should there be an IPO. A doubtful reward, I suppose. I passed that on to Uber as a potential retention incentive. No response was forthcoming.

What is even more astounding to me than the number of Uber rides I have given, but the real likelihood that I had more than thirty-thousand riders in my car!

GPS and Uber

Global Positioning Satellites (GPS) are essential to the functioning of the whole Uber ride-sharing app. As soon as a ride is requested, Uber's computers merge GPS technology to determine both where the rider is and the location of the nearest driver whose app is simultaneously open. The nearest driver is "pinged"; the driver accepts the request and proceeds to the GPS location of the rider. Well, that's how it's supposed to work.

But, as anyone who has driven for Uber, or for anyone who has requested an Uber ride knows: the system is not perfect. In some cases, the match-ups can be way off; sometimes miles off. The array of 24-33 satellites and ground stations in the USA GPS system is pretty accurate within nine meters so why the errors?

Most of the anomalies where drivers can't find PAX and, conversely, riders are perplexed in not seeing their driver where they expect them are situations involving wrong data. For example, a person sitting in a restaurant, say with an address of 20 Elm Street, may be in the back of that establishment that is very close to an address one block over. In that case, the passenger used "current location" as the pick-up point. GPS reads that not by the address, but by the proximity of the site which is next to an address on another street.

Using huge databases, such as found in Google Maps™, are more a more reliable way of stating a location than simply requesting "current location." That is, is a would be passenger specifies 20 Elm Street, or even Frankie's Restaurant, the Google Maps database coordinates with GPS to provide that location and the directions to the driver for getting there.

The worst human errors in pick-up locations occur when a new user of Uber tries to move the pin in the app to specify their location. On that tiny screen be it Android or IPhone, a fraction of a fraction of an inch movement can result in the pick-up location being a mile or more off.

Uber currently gives drivers the choice of using either Uber's own proprietary navigation system or Google Maps. As of this writing, Uber's navigation is horribly inaccurate. My riders accept my apology for Uber when the app's voice directions specify a right turn when their own map shows left and vice-versa. Many times the overall routes are simply inaccurate. If it weren't for the fact that I have driven 10,000 rides and know Asheville navigation several times every night. pretty darn well, I would be led astray by Uber's

A comment I make that usually elicits hearty laughs from my passengers goes, "I have a theory that Kelly Ann Conway left the Trump White House for her new job: She replaced Siri as the voice of Uber navigation and now gives us *alternative facts and alternative directions.* They are clearly wrong and have to be ignored if we are to get to our destinations!"

When I am in areas new to me, I invariably switch over from the Uber Navigation, which seems like an underdeveloped beta-test, to the mostly reliable Google system. "No, no, Kelly Ann, that is NOT the way to Highland Brewing Company!"

Uber is Dangerous?

Recently there have been stories of law suits that add to the negative press that seem magnetic to Uber. In one case apparently, there is a pending class action suit that complains that Uber is not safe for riders and should have more regulation to make it so.

Speaking as both a consumer of Uber service as well as a driver, I cannot see why Uber's ride-share experience should be any more, or less, dangerous than other forms of ground transportation.

First, consider the fact that Uber does a background check on its drivers. No felons are allowed; nobody with DUI convictions in five years; no cars that will not pass inspection.

Next consider the information provided in the app that is readily available to a passenger. In what other ground transportation service do you have the name of the driver; means to contact them directly by phone or text; and even a little personal information including their picture. The prospective passenger and also see the number of rides the driver has given and the rating that driver has. Would anyone have access to that

kind of information for taxicabs, car service, bus, or shuttle van?
Of course, not!

Even so, I get comments about the service from, perhaps, new users who are somewhat afraid of "getting into a car with a stranger." Given what was just said above, I usually just laugh it off with the comment, "So, you know and trust cab drivers more than Uber?"

With millions of people driving for Uber world-wide there are no doubt a few instances of murders and rape committed by Uber drivers. These infrequent crimes rise up quickly in the international press and internet globally, but are likely more rare than similar horrors committed in demographics much smaller than the aggregate of the Uber driving population.

As sensational as the bad news of bad behavior of a tiny minority of Uber drivers can be, it must be noted that perpetrators can be apprehended very quickly within the record of the app. Actually, every single ride on Uber is stored in a massive database that includes every aspect of an individual ride with a Google Maps™ of that specific trip.

All that said, it is worth reminding riders that they should only get in an Uber car that they have requested after verifying the driver's name. They also need to hear from the driver their own name and confirm the destination to which the driver shows to be accurate.

There have been instances, very rare indeed, of Uber impersonators showing up to pick up people with whom they have no business. That is a crime in itself and could be the beginning of something worse. If the right Uber car is marked as an Uber car, has a verifiable driver; has the right name and destination, then it is likely100% safe to get in that car.

Despite all the safeguards built into the app, there was a terrible tragedy in Columbia, South Carolina when a USC coed got into a car that was not her Uber car. She was murdered! After that, Uber and Lyft made some more improvements to safety features such as ride tracking.

The North Carolina legislature passed a law effective January 1, 2020 requiring the license plate number of Uber and Lyft cars to display the number on the front wind shield.

Dangerous Situation Avoided

One night as I approached my pick-up location, near Ben's Tune UP, I saw a small crowd of young men yelling and shoving one another. I hoped none of them were my fare.

Unfortunately, three of the protagonists were looking for me. They correctly identified that Frank was the one paying, so I welcomed them into the car. Yelling out the window of my car continued for about half a block.

For the next twenty minutes I heard their version of the altercation which seemed to have involved a female, name calling, and the differences in what guys from Boston (them) and the locals considered to be offensive.

Somebody was called a "fat leprechaun" whose date was called that person's mother that one of my pax said he had sex with...rather "f**ked."

Then they went on at some length about who would have won the fight if a punch had been thrown. Apparently there were eight locals versus the three from Boston. One said he could have taken the leprechaun and the "skinny one" but he thought the "Big Dude in the Plaid Shirt" might have been a problem.

They then played out various scenarios most of which resulted in them winning the fight, but also going to jail.

The more sober of the three concluded that my arrival for their Lyft pick-up saved them from going to jail.

"Mom" to the Rescue

    A female rider, Joan, told me this story: A woman, Shirley, driving for Uber in Boston picked her up for a ride to Logan Airport. Shirley is a middle-aged lady with a strong Boston accent. She's a big woman; at least 200 pounds on a 5'10" frame. Joan asked, "What was it like being a woman driving for Uber especially at night" and "Have you had any wild rides?" Joan asked.

    "Well, I guess you would have to say so," was Shirley's reply. "One night I picked up a completely intoxicated young man, I'll call him "Brad." It was very late one night in Roxbury.

    "Almost immediately after getting in my car, Brad passed out. It was a fairly long ride to Brad's apartment out there in Acton. I thought Brad would wake up before we got to Acton, but he didn't."

    "Hey, Brad, wake up!" I yelled, but got no response from Brad. This kid is half my age, alright?"

    Shirley said, "I opened the back passenger door and Brad nearly fell out, but still, I couldn't wake him.

"So, what did you do?" Joan asked

" Well, I pulled him out and laid him on the sidewalk. He looked so pitiful! He could barely stand up! I helped get him up the steps to his apartment. He got his keys out, but couldn't get them in the lock. I took his keys and opened the door. He slumped over and almost fell off the stoop."

"Jeez, Shirley, what happened then?" Joan asked, mouth agape.

"I lifted him up. He was kinda skinny; maybe 130 pounds. I practically carried up the steps to his apartment. He got his keys out but couldn't make them work. I helped and got him inside. Then I took him to his bedroom and tucked him in his bed."

"Really?" an astonished Joan questioned. "Why did you do that?"

"I guess Brad just reminded me so much of my son," Shirley replied, laughing.

Still Kickin'

Early on a Wednesday evening I had a pick-up at a nursing home. Usually, it is a visitor not a resident of the home that is my passenger. Doris, a short doughty woman in her eighties, said she lived there.

"Where to Doris?" I asked.

"I was going to go to church, but I changed my mind." I was aware of Wednesday night services at Baptist churches so that was not surprising; her new destination: her karate lessons!

After putting in the address of the new destination, Fletcher Martial Arts Academy, I said,
"That's cool, Doris! How long have you been doing that?"

"About three years."

"Do you have your Black Belt yet?" I asked in all seriousness.

Doris said, "I would have but the night they gave the Black Belt test, I got in the wrong line."
"You got in the wrong line?" I asked for clarification.

"Yes, my instructor, Nick, had shown me a way I could kick a board in half; with my heel, not my toes. But I got in Tonya's line, not Nick's and when I told her that Nick showed me a new way to kick the board, but Tonya said. 'Doris we can't make no exceptions for nobody'. That's why I don't have a Black Belt. Got to kick a board in half.

"Well," I said, "you are still kickin' and next time be sure Nick is your judge!"

Conflict Resolution

Occasionally drivers get in the middle of some sort of dispute. A rider will ask the driver to take a side. This is not recommended, but sometimes unavoidable.

One evening a driver picked up three guys in their forties and one younger woman, probably in her late twenties. They said they were going to party at one of the guys houses.

It was a fairly long trip and on the way a dispute arose. The driver did not catch the reason for the conflict and had no intention of intervening despite the fact that he was a psychology major and had some experience in conflict resolution.

His reluctance to stay out of it ended when the woman said to one of the men, "I'm going to punch you in the face!"

Another man, Bob, the ride-payer, grabbed the woman's arm, saying "Hey, Angel, don't hurt my buddy!"

Angel said, "I'm going to kick his ass!"

The driver said, "Hey, ya'll! Just cool it. We are all friends here, right? Whatever you may be thinking at this moment, will pass. Now let's show each other some love and I'll get you where we're going."

They immediately stopped fighting and arguing. After a few moments of silence, Angel raised up her sweater revealing her ample breasts. The guys began touching her treasures like children at a petting zoo.

I guess that was Angel's interpretation of "showing some love."

Conflict resolution skills came to good use that night!

Moon Shot

Weddings are such an important part of Uber business in Asheville it isn't surprising that many rides involve getting bachelorettes to and from venues, bars, etc.

I believe there must be a *Bachelorette Play Book* that calls for extremely loud talking; mostly gossip about other girls; and the prerequisite of doing something crazy as to be memorable or notorious.

So, one night I was driving a longer ride out beyond the Fairview community southwest of town. On the way, the girls see the other Uber car that was transporting more of their party. Apparently, the bride to be was in the other car on the five lane part of US 74. My bachelorettes wanted me to race the other car. I refused. Then they asked me to pull along side of the other car. With the windows down, they started screaming.

If that wasn't bad enough, they decided for a Girls Gone Wild "mooning." One girl removed her panties and stuck her butt in the window. The moon shot was effective. The other driver blew his horn; I blew mine and the incident passed with peals of laughter.

Poachers

Sometimes, thankfully rare, the wrong rider will get in an Uber car or the Uber driver will pick up the wrong passengers. Either way, the result is the same: somebody did not get picked up and that person is the one paying for the ride. This is a real mess that can be straightened out, but not without some effort on the driver's part to make the correction.

Errors such as this happen when the driver does not confirm the identity of the rider and/or the passenger has not confirmed they have the right driver and car.

Even with those checks in place there have been instances of "ride poaching." I am referring here to fraud, a misdemeanor, wherein a person who has not requested an Uber ride gets in a car claiming to be the person who ordered the ride. They get away with the fraud unless the driver asks to verify his or her name.

Such was the case when some students needed a ride and were cavalier enough to hop in my waiting car. One claimed to be "Sam" which I had given away by asking if he was Sam.

"Yep, that's me," the Not-Really-Sam replied. His partners in crime thought that was funny.

"So you are heading up to Asheville Brew?" I confirmed as the destination.

"No we need to get back to campus," Not-Really-Sam replied. (Again, more laughter from the back seat.)

At that point the smell of a rat was getting intense. "Okay," I said pulling over on a darkened part of Broadway Street. "Everybody out, now! You aren't 'Sam' and you have poached somebody else's ride. Get out now!"

They all got out and I had to go back, find the real Sam and take him to Asheville Brew. Then I had to do a fare adjustment. That was enough of a hassle to cure me of not being careful enough in confirming the identity of the PAX.

Third Party Passenger

A driver in Philadelphia received a request from a man named Robert. Nothing seemed unusual about the trip until the man revealed that the trip was not for him, but for "a friend."

Such third party trips are also fairly common. In those cases there's an opportunity to get a rider referral for which Uber pays a driver $5.00 and gives the new first-time rider a free ride using the provided code. The driver giving the free ride gets the normal fare from Uber so it's a win-win deal.

In this particular case the passenger was not capable of accepting the referral and lacked the credit card necessary to sign up for an account. The reason was due to the fact that the third party passenger was an inflated sex doll in the actual size of a naked woman.

The man paying for the trip had an address for delivery of "Dolly." Still, it was pretty weird driving through downtown streets with a sex toy in the front passenger seat.

Upon arrival at the designated drop off place was a real woman. She said, "What the fuck is this?"

The driver said, "Robert sent her."

The woman said, "Mother Fucker! Send it back!"

"I can't do that without an Uber ride request," the driver replied.

"I don't have Uber on my phone."

"I can help with that. Go to the app on Google Play or the Apple Store. Follow the directions when it comes up enter the code here (giving her his card)."

The third party referral worked after all and the doll was returned at least as far as the street corner where Dolly was picked up.

Third Party Disaster

I heard this Uber tale from a guy in a bar where I was taking a break and having a Coke ...a downside of driving for Uber is not having a beer! When he learned that I was an Uber driver he said, "I gotta tell you about what happened to me: So, I live in Baltimore. My buddies and I came out of a bar. My friend ordered an Uber. While we were waiting, we see this chick across the street lying on a sidewalk. We went over there and she was not bad looking and didn't look homeless.

She woke up and cried. Said she needed to get home. Said she had no money and didn't have Uber either.

My Uber driver arrived and I thought I would be a Good Samaritan and let her have the car I ordered. We were in a busy area and my buddy called for another ride.

The next day an Uber charge popped up for the ride I gave to that drunk chick. She went way outside Baltimore County. There was a surge on and the tab was over $900!"

My comment, "Third party Uber rides can be a disaster."

A Very Special Uber Ride

In Charleston, South Carolina, an older Asian man is an Uber driver who offers his riders a unique experience.

When passengers got in Mr. Ho's car everything seemed normal at first. Then the tiny lights that were all over the headliner in the car made an instant constellation. The pax thought they were in Bailey's "Cash Cab," a popular reality show that featured Ben Bailey as the driver of a cab that had a trivia contest for the passengers who chose to participate. Right answers won them money; wrong ones resulted in being ousted from the cab short of their destination. The show ran for twelve years 2005-2017.

In Charleston, there was no trivia contest, but rather a sophisticated karaoke set-up. Mr. Ho had few words to say just, "Pick any song you like."

Since there were three young male riders, they said, "Backstreet Boys. *I Want It That Way.*"

Mr. Ho offered a microphone. The song appeared on a nine inch screen on Mr. Ho's dashboard.

Three imitation Back Street Boys crooned the words as they appeared on the screen.

The guy who told me this story said that the experience was unforgettable. I promised to include it in *Uber & Out.*

Another Expensive Uber Ride

Back in my hometown, Morgantown, West Virginia, a couple of young men went a convenience store. The more inebriated of the two went into the store where there was a long line of beer purchasing customers.

The guy who went in for the beer told his buddy, Kenny, to wait and said he'd be "right back."

Apparently, a somewhat wasted Kenny got tired of waiting and called an Uber.

The driver quickly arrived and picked the passenger up. Looking at the destination, the driver exclaimed, "Wow, that's a long ride!"

"That's ok if you're ok with it," Kenny replied. "Just take me home."

Kenny went to sleep in back seat. The driver touched the navigation tab in the app and off they went into the night.

The 'home' destination was for an address in Fairfield, New Jersey, some 300+ miles from Morgantown.

Six hours later, the driver said, "Here we are, Kenny." It was Kenny's home address which he had specified, not his temporary residence in Morgantown.

"Oh, shit! Really?" a now fully wake Kenny exclaimed.

The ride was on a so-called 'surge' price and Kenny's account got charged $1,636.00.

Kenny tried to get money back from Uber for his mistake, but ultimately the charge stuck.

A Good Long Ride

One night last June I was called to one of the housing projects to pick up Phil. I know that several of my driver colleagues will not go to the "ghettoes" due to the high crime rates there. I go because I know poor people depend on Uber and Lyft to get places and refusals add to misery in many cases.

When I arrived at the pick-up I was a bit surprised that the pax was white. Ninety percent of the people living there are black. Not only was "Phil" white it turned out he wasn't Phil. He was Adam. We do not see where somebody is going to until we pick them up.

Adam, said, "Can you take me to Georgia?"

I had started the trip and quickly saw the address was a hospital in Riverdale, GA; about 25 miles south of Atlanta. I hadn't seen my son in Atlanta in several months, I agreed to the ride.

On the 240 mile ride I learned that Adam's cousin, Phil, had ordered the ride for him. Adam had had some really bad luck.

A former resident of Asheville, Adam had decided to return to live here. He had packed up everything he owned into his SUV and drove up from Atlanta. Adam parked in front of a convenience store along the highway near Asheville. Adam said, "I wasn't in there more than five minutes, and damn! Somebody stole my car!"

"That's awful!" I sympathized. "Did they catch him?"

"No, that's why I needed this ride. They did get his picture on a surveillance camera. He looked like a thief. All tattooed. Walked around the car, saw the keys dangling there; jumped in and drove off. I wish he had just taken the car. I had my guitar in there which I like more than the car."

"Damn, that's bad luck," I said.

"That's not all. I called my brother to tell him about that. He didn't call me back. Come to find out from Phil that my bro is in the hospital in Riverdale. He was in a car wreck!"

"Well, glad I can be of some help." I spent the night at my son's house. It was the week before Father's Day. He and his wife took me to a great brunch late Sunday morning.

The Innocent Mule

I heard this story from another Asheville driver in response to the usual question, "What's the longest ride you have had."

Frank said, "My longest was Asheville to Florida. Actually, that was all the way to St. Augustine."

"Jeez...you got me beat! That's got to be 500 miles."

"Right. I used to live in Jacksonville. I called my friend who still lives there and he said I could stay with him a while after the trip."

Frank told his tale: "When Ramon, my passenger, got to my car he put two boxes and a duffle bag into the trunk. He said he had to take some stuff to his brother. We stopped several times so it took over nine hours. We drove all night, listening to music and telling our life stories to each other."

Frank continued "When we got into St. Augustine, close to the drop-off,

Ramon says 'do you know what I have in those boxes?' "No, so what's in the boxes?"

"A kilo of cocaine in one; and that much meth in the other."

"Shit!" I said, "God Almighty! I could go to jail for a long time just for being your delivery boy!"

"Calm down, Frank," Ramon said in a matter-of-fact way. "Don't worry we are almost there. I am just screwin' with you."

"So I took Ramon to a house in a low rent part of St. Augustine. He got out, got his stuff from the trunk, and handed me a nice $100 bill as a tip. The ride itself paid $289."

"I went to my friends place at 8 AM. That night we were watching the news that there had been a drug bust that morning. And, no shit, the house that got busted was the same place I dropped off Ramon! I was freakin' out thinkin' the cops had that house under surveillance and might have my car on tape."

I said, "Wow, what a story! You were an innocent drug mule!"

Surge Pricing

I sometimes hear from my passengers complaining about having to pay exorbitant prices for Uber rides. While I am sympathetic to their concerns, I do explain how that works and what to do about it. "What to do about it" does not mean getting a refund.

"Surge," that is, high demand pricing, is based on a computer algorithm that counts the number of potential customers in a given area with the number of drivers near to serve them. If the proportion is higher than a predetermined normal ratio, the surge goes in effect. That could be anywhere to, say, 25% more than the standard fare to, I have seen, 10 times the usual fare. It is not unusual, for example, for a fare to run over $100 for a fairly short ride across town on New Year's Eve.

Lyft has the same sort of price increase mechanism. They call theirs "Prime Time." Both say the systems encourage drivers to go to the zone of high demand with the incentive they get from the increased fares. Drivers get the same percentage of a fare no matter how high the fare.

What can you do about surge pricing? Since I am a user of Uber myself, I can offer a bit of consumer advice:

wait until the surge passes. Go have another beer. Try later. Of course, if you are in a hurry, go ahead and pay the higher cost. Chances are fairly good that your ride will still cost less than a taxicab.

In any case, you can check the cost of a ride before you make the request. At least one app shows a comparison of Lyft to Uber. Usually both have Surge or Prime Time going on at the same time, but not always, so there's another possibility for avoiding high demand costs.

Uber+1?

In addition to the standard "Uber X," a normal 4 door sedan seating 5 including the driver, Uber offers bigger cars, Uber XL, and, some cities, special cars such as "Uber Black Car" for folks who need to be impressive riding in a black BMW, Cadillac, Mercedes, or other expensive vehicle. These are ordered by people with lots of money, or by people pretending they have lots of money, or maybe, guys trying to impress a Prom date.

Since the Asheville market is relatively small, here you will only find Uber X and Uber XL.

Coby Persin, a driver in Miami, has made a YouTube video in which he surprises his pax by driving up in a Lamborghini *Avantador*. That's a supercar not approved by Uber, but pretty cool, nonetheless. Coby signed up with Uber with a Ford Fusion which is what people expect when Coby shows up. He simply says, "You get a Lamborghini today" and the delighted passengers get in.

In the video, you'll see happy passengers taking selfies of the experience. In one he picks up a dog at a hotel to be delivered somewhere in Miami. The big golden retriever also seems delighted to have the wind in his face.

I wondered what would happen if Coby got to a pick-up spot and more than one passenger needed the ride. Coby thought of that. A back up car (his Ford Fusion or another Uber) was following to cover him. You see the couple going in separate cars; the guy's date gets in the supercar.

I don't think Uber has given their approval of sports cars whether super or not and one wonders if Uber has seen the video and what, if anything, they did about it

Even before seeing Coby's Lamborghini video, I had the idea to proposing to Uber that they have a category called "Uber+1" which would be a sports car alternative. I have a Mazda MX5 Miata. I think there would be interest for one rider in being picked up in such a car especially in Asheville on a beautiful day or night. There would no doubt be interest in Corvettes, Smart Cars, tiny electric vehicles and so on.

Free Advice

I don't know if it's my appearance, grey and wrinkled, that causes younger Uber riders to ask me if I have any advice for them. The question usually comes on a long ride and involves love life. No, it is not young women seeking that advice. It is always young men. They are trying to understand a female partner. I confess to having little to say about that as women have always been a mystery that eludes my understanding.

Nevertheless, I offer the wisdom that one of my first sales managers shared with me and other young men about to go on the road for a living. I call this bit of free advice, "Fred's Rules of the Road."

- Never eat at a place called "Mom's."
- Never play cards with a man named "Doc."
- Never go to bed with anyone whose problems are worse than your own.

Over the years I have found these as good as any other words to live by.

Tipping

Long ago an established taxicab tradition was that of tipping. When it first started, Uber promoted itself as a "no tipping" service. The implication was that driver's pay was fair. The service cost far less than cabs already and the absence of tips made it even more so.

But many riders, not the majority, but many, want to give a tip to the driver because they feel the service was exceptional; the music was great; or the driver was helpful in making dining or other recommendations. I often feel like a tour guide or concierge even making reservations for people that want them. All these are ample reasons for getting a tip. Some PAX want to give a tip, but have no cash to do so—at least that's how it was when Uber did not have tipping on the credit card on the Uber account.

Lyft had the tipping capability on their accounts from the day they started, about a year after Uber. In 2017 Uber amended their app and policy to allow for tipping on the card on file.

I do not know how my tips stack up against other driver's tips. I cannot ever know when I will or will not get a tip unless the rider tells me that is their intention. Even then I can't predict the size of the tip. "On card" tips range from $2.00 to $10.00. Once in a blue moon I will get an exceptionally large tip. I have had several for $20 and even a $50 one.

A recent survey of Uber tipping practices showed that only 62% of passengers tip Uber drivers. In my experience that seems high. The same survey revealed that male passengers are 23% more likely to tip than females.

I have tried to see a correlation between my behavior and the tips I get. I think I am just as helpful and charming on nights that I get no tips as those when I get $60.

Also there seems to be no predicting which passengers will tip and those who don't. I have had big tips from rough looking country folk and nothing from well-heeled rich people staying in $400 per night hotels. The most consistent tippers are the average servers and bartenders whose livelihoods depend on tips.

They call that "tipping karma" with the act of tipping practically guaranteeing more tips for themselves.

A Gambler's Tips

Years ago, in the days before Uber, I took many taxi rides. Once, on the way to a sales meeting in Las Vegas, I was picked up by Cedric, a tanned and grizzled veteran of cab driving in Vegas.

On the way to my hotel, Cedric and I engaged in the usual chit-chat about what I'm doing here and how long he's been a cabbie, etc.

I asked Cedric who had been in Vegas forty years if he gambled.

Cedric said, "Well, sometimes I do.   Never won much."

"So, Cedric, do you have any tips on winning?"   I asked, hoping for some seasoned advice from a native.

Cedric began, "Show me somebody who thinks they are on a winning streak and I will show you a loser. And if somebody is on a losing streak and thinks they are close to winning, I'll show you another loser."

"Ok, so you are saying there's no way to win at gambling?" I wondered. "Or do you have a strategy for winning? You must have something to say about that since you said that you do gamble occasionally."

"Yes, I do," Cedric replied. ""Here's what you need to do: First take a hundred dollars, maybe more, but that must be money that you absolutely don't need. It's 'fun money;' just for the entertainment. That money is your *stake*. Next, you need to set a time of the day or night that you are going to quit. Don't stay at a table a minute longer than you planned. Keep your stake in one pocket of your pants or coat. In another pocket have a stamped, self addressed, envelope."

"What's that for?" I asked.

"The envelope is for your winnings." Cedric replied. "Never gamble with winnings! Just gamble with your stake; that's the money you didn't care to lose, remember? When your time is up, walk out. Put that envelope in the nearest mailbox. When you get home, you'll have some money waiting for you."

Uber: the Movie

I often get great review comments on the music I play. My car came with a really great XFinity sound system and all genres of music sound really good on it. One night last spring I happened to be playing some Indian music. I always ask my passengers if they want to hear something else no matter what I happen to be listening to at the time. On that night *Karunesh's Evening Reflections* was on. My two male passengers said they liked it.

I said, "Thanks. I usually have on Pandora the latest band playing at the Orange Peel. Last night that was *Old Crow Medicine Show*." That band was a sell-out at "the Peel" two nights running.

The tranquil Indian music was a nice change from the all American sound of Old Crow. I said this kind of sounds like a sound-track from some Bollywood film.

One of the riders said, "Yeah, I should make a Bollywood movie right now."

With directing suggestions from his friend, the guy whipped out his Iphone X and started making a video. "Pan over there!" He said as the nightscape of Asheville flashed by. "Zoom onto those people walking. Use slo-mo, etc."

All the while I drove them the ten minutes from West Asheville to their stop downtown, he continued filming. The Bollywood soundtrack played in the background. Maybe *Uber: the Movie* will show up on YouTube?

Uber 24/7

A young man, Phil, with a Prius drives for Uber in Wilmington, NC. One night he got a long ride to Raleigh. Rides like that are usually profitable even if the driver returns home empty of passengers.

Since Phil was already in Raleigh, he decided to stay and kept Ubering. When it was really late, around 4:00 AM he was too tired to drive back to Wilmington. He spent the rest of the night sleeping in his car. When he woke up, about noon, he continued driving in the Raleigh and Durham, NC area.

Then he had an idea: why not just stay here? He had membership in a nationwide gym and went in one for a shower. Phil picked up a change of clothes at Wal-Mart and kept on driving. He was waiting for an Uber trip to Wilmington, but instead took the next long one to Greensboro, North Carolina.

After spending a couple of weeks in the "Triad" (Winston-Salem, Greensboro, and Highpoint area), he got a ride request to Asheville where has also worked several weeks.

Uber allows drivers to work 60 hours a week where after they need to take at least 24 hours off. The Wilmington driver says he is "on call 24/7" since he sleeps in his car and is ready anytime a request comes through.

Phillip is one of only two Uber drivers I know of that make around $60-75,000 per year Ubering. The other is a former long-distance truck driver who used to go back and forth from the East Coast to California every week. I met him at a Waffle House having dinner, as I was, at 2:00 AM. He said he works 60-70 hours a week and earns over $60,000 doing so. That, he said, was about what he made as a trucker, but now he could be home every night.

After taking heat from authorities for allowing drivers to have unlimited time behind the wheel, both Uber and Lyft will allow drivers to work "only" twelve hours at a stretch after which they must be off the clock for six hours. Of course, by driving for both Uber and Lyft as I and many drivers do, it is possible to work 24/7 by simply closing one app and starting the other. If I were a Skin Walker, perhaps I could do that? Not!

Accident Prone

One afternoon I picked up "Annabelle" at an automotive body shop where she had dropped off her car for some major repairs.

She said, "I hydroplaned on a wet and winding road in North Asheville near my house. You'll see the tree I hit when you drive me home."

In the course of the fairly long ride to her place, Annabelle told me stories of other accidents she had been involved in: "The car I just wrecked was the replacement for one that was totaled. That accident was not my fault. My boyfriend was driving my car and we were stopped behind a huge flatbed truck. A tractor-trailer semi came over the hill behind us and ran right over us and drove us under the flatbed. Our car was nearly flattened. I ended up in the backseat in a ball. My friend actually walked away from it---I don't know how. I had multiple broken bones. I have a lot of pins and screws in me!"

"Good Lord!" I replied, "It's a wonder both of you weren't killed."

"That's what everyone says. And I had been involved in nine other pretty serious accidents. And I'm just 32!"

"The only good news was that big trucking companies have really good insurance. I came out with $100,000. Got my Ford Fusion with that and made a pretty good down payment on my house. A still have pain, though, and need to go for physical therapy once a week."

"That sounds like you might have settled for not enough money?" I suggested.

"Probably," Annabelle replied. "You know, I thought about driving for Uber. I like people, but I am now too scared to drive very much. I think I am accident prone."

As we passed a large de-barked tree on the left side of the road that had been skinned by her Ford Fusion, "Probably," was my reply.

Wild Kingdom

Asheville is known mostly for the many tourist attractions, restaurants, breweries, music, and arts to be found here as well as for being close to nature for hiking and seeing waterfalls. It is also home to every species of mammal and bird found in the mountains and forests that embrace her.

The North Carolina Wildlife Service has identified more than one hundred and fifty black bears within the city limits! Many of the bears have been tagged with GPS tracking collars. One young male bear was tracked all the way from Asheville to Bryson City, NC, some sixty miles west. He stayed there a year, and then returned to Asheville. He was either homesick, or, perhaps, found the garbage more abundant and tasty in the bigger city?

One Valentine's Day evening a very large female deer bounded out right in front of my car in front of Asheville High School which is less than a mile from downtown. I had not even a second to react and the impact with the doe all but destroyed my car. She appeared to be pregnant which made me very sad. A man helped me move her off the roadway onto a sidewalk. I made my way home with one remaining headlight and took another car back to the site of accident. I wanted to take a picture for insurance, but in less than thirty minutes she had disappeared, apparently just stunned by the impact. Repairs ran to nearly $5,000, luckily covered by comprehensive insurance.

In addition to the foxes, raccoons, rabbits, possums, squirrels, groundhogs, and various other rodents that I see on a nightly basis while out Ubering, we have a recent arrival in our Wild Kingdom: Coyotes.

Coyotes are an "invasive species" that have migrated to Western North Carolina from the west. They have become quite numerous, nobody knows how many, though nearly everyone I talk to about them has seen at least one within the past year. And they kill domestic pets.

My vet says coyotes are known to have killed many small dogs and any size cat in Asheville. I know of two they got: one of a neighbor's and one of my own cats. One of my PAX actually witnessed a coyote catching a cat.

Black bears are everywhere in Asheville. They have been in the parking garage at the mall. One bear was seen sitting there holding a discarded milkshake cup from a nearby fast food restaurant. On a warm late spring day, one came in through the large open doors at Asheville High while classes were still in session.

The school was put on "lockdown" until the bear was shooed out. While scary to a lot of people, black bears are timid creatures. The only time they are dangerous is when they have cubs and somebody accidently gets between mom and her babies.

One campground on the Blue Ridge Parkway which runs through South and
East Asheville had to be closed due the presence of bears in and around the tables and tents (with people inside) probably looking for food. I think they weren't looking for humans to eat, but the rangers closed the camp anyway until the spring birthing season had passed.

Another ubiquitous sight in Asheville are the wild turkeys that used to be fairly rare in town. Now, it seems, everyone has them. My flock, that is, the regulars to my yard, numbers seventeen. The huge tom turkeys are magnificent, spreading their tail feathers and puffing out their iridescent chests to impress the hens seeming to care less as they go about pecking for seeds on the yard.

One night I was Ubering a couple out to the Inn on Biltmore Estate. In that four mile ride we saw several deer including a majestic looking eight-point buck. One the same ride we also saw a fairly large black bear and a red fox.

The guy from Ohio said, "I am 45 years old and that is the first bear I have ever seen in the wild." His wife chimed in, "Yeah, that's my first bear and fox, too!"

On top of seeing the Biltmore House, going to several breweries, and having had a great meal at a five star restaurant, seeing a little of Asheville's Wild Kingdom may have been the most memorable event of their visit.
Bearly Alive

One night I picked up a hiker, not a hitch-hiker; he did have an Uber account. "Jake" was a long-distance hiker. He said, "I've done two-thousand miles in the past year."

"Wow, that's impressive! Where have you been?"

"California, Oregon, Utah. After North Carolina, I'm hooking up with friends an doing trails in West Virginia."

Jake said he really liked the "Green East, the waterfalls, and the whitewater rivers."

He was well aware of the several deaths that have unfortunately occurred in Western North Carolina already this year. He said, "You have to really be careful when the water is up, but actually, all of the time. Most of those accidents could have been avoided if the victims had just obeyed warning signs and used common sense."

I asked Jake if had ever had a close call or been in a dangerous situation. He had:

"Not with water, but with a bear," Jake replied.

"Like in the movie, *Revenant*?" I asked.

"Not that bad!" Jake laughed. "I had put my food stash in a bag and suspended it high in a tree near my tent. You are supposed to loop a rope over a high limb and then lower it down where it's still twelve or fifteen feet off the ground and, maybe, ten feet below the tree limb. Well, I heard a noise in the night and peeked out of my tent.

A bear was up in the tree. He went out on the limb and pulled my food bag up. He ripped the bag off and then went back to the ground, picked up my bag and ran off. I was too scared to care about the food and didn't make a sound.

The bad part was the next morning when I was hungry. I checked my maps and I was 22 miles from Damascus, Virginia. I had been eating very little to conserve my supply of trail mix and protein bars. Now I had nothing. Five hours later I was feeling like I was starving. I had no cell phone connection. I felt like I was in one of those reality survivor shows. There were no berries to eat; too early for that.

Luckily, that afternoon, I heard rustling down the mountain and it was not another bear. It was another hiker. He had enough food to share. We had a good laugh and made it to that nearest town by dark."

Lost in the Woods

One night, about 8:30 on a chilly Spring night I had a ping for a pick up on Ox Creek Road which connects the farmland below to the Blue Ridge Mountains. There were very few houses on that road and the dense woods are actually part of the scenic Blue Ridge Parkway.

Thanks to GPS, which was still working even in that remote area, I found a shivering couple along the road.

"Oh, thank God!" the woman exclaimed as they got in the car. "We were lost in the woods!"

Her boyfriend explained, "Yeah, thank God! We parked our car on the Parkway at 5:30. Guess that was stupid to start hiking through the woods then? The trail disappeared and we hit a spot with no cell service. We kept walking. It got dark. Michelle was about to cry when the GPS came back up. We also had a map that showed where Ox Creek Road was. And we called for an Uber."

"Well, I am happy to be your rescuer." I said, "Now let's find your car."

Michelle said, "I was so scared. I heard there are lots of bears around here."

"Yep, there are, I said. "And they are all fond of frozen meat!"

We all laughed.

Uber and a Hitchhiker

Many years ago, say fifty, in a country that had fewer problems (or we just didn't know about them before the internet) many people including kids would hitchhike everywhere. In 1965 I hitchhiked to California from West Virginia. And I knew a girl, a cheerleader at my high school, who hitchhiked to the Jersey Shore from Morgantown to her summer job as a lifeguard. People thought that was resourceful and brave, but no one thought she was foolish or crazy. It was just a way to travel back then.

Now, the practice of hitchhiking is very uncommon because it is commonly believed that it is crazy and dangerous to pick up a hitchhiker or even to be a hitchhiker.

So a story is going around, unverified, that an Uber driver was going home late one night. He was not interested in doing any more Uber rides and had turned off his app. But he saw a forlorn looking hitchhiker and, remembering the old days when he give and get hitching ride, decided to pick him up.

When they had driven a mile in silence after the initial greeting, the hitchhiker spoke up, "Hey, thanks for picking me up. I was thinking, how would you know that I wasn't a serial killer?"

The Uber driver responded with a grin, "No I wasn't worried about that. After all, what are the chances of TWO serial killers being in the same car?"

Sense of Urgency

One late afternoon I picked up three men at Sierra Nevada Brewery. That East Coast operation of the nationally well-known brand is located south of the Asheville Airport in a beautifully landscaped site along Mills River. The building itself with its striking "mountain lodge" architecture makes this one of the biggest new tourist attraction in the area.

The men had flown in from Florida in their own charter plane piloted by one of the men. "Paul" was the pilot. He was also a commercial pilot doing cross country flights on a regular basis.

They had been at Sierra Nevada most of the afternoon sampling many of the beers in the SN lineup. As we were heading north to the destination in downtown Asheville, Paul said, "Can you take me to a gas station? I need to pee."

"Sure" I said, "there's one on the way."

Well, anyone coming into Asheville on almost any afternoon will encounter a massive traffic jam. Mostly it's just a bulge caused by never-ending road construction on I-26. Sometimes there's an accident which really shuts things down for many minutes.

At first, Paul said, "Good, I can wait." But as the wait grew longer, Paul said he was feeling "a sense or urgency."
One of Paul's friends asked him if he had his "Pilot's Depends" on. Something new I had never heard of: apparently pilots often wear absorbent underpants to avoid the need to go to the head. They just answer the call of nature without having to leave control of the plane.

I pulled over off the interstate as soon as I could, but not before Paul had a leakage. He ran into some bushes to relieve himself. There was a large wet spot on the front of his shorts. When he returned to the car he said, "Whew. That was close! At least I didn't pee on your leather seats! I am so used to going when I have a sense of urgency, I just go. Maybe I need to see a doctor?"

"Yeah, maybe," I answered, "but be sure to tell him about the 47 beers you drank at Sierra Nevada."

Pet Peeves of Uber Drivers

Every Uber driver I know has a list of bad behaviors, or pet peeves, that challenge one's patience and temper. I try my best not to seem irritated even when I am. I have to say to myself, "Your passengers may be difficult or obnoxious, or just ignorant about the Uber app, but they are here to enjoy themselves and this great place to visit." That's my advice to all my colleagues as well: Be Tolerant.

That said, I have a short list of things not to do as a passenger for Uber:

#1. Getting sick. If you feel sick, let the driver know. He or she will pull over and let you out to vomit by the road so you don't foul the car with your spew. Uber, by the way, does charge a pax up to $150 for a clean-up. This has happened to me only once, but it was a Saturday night and I could not not drive until the mess was cleaned up. $150 was not enough compensation. I can detect likely pukers, and have on several occasions pulled over to accommodate them on the side of the road.

#2. Smoking in an Uber car. Some drivers allow "vaping," but most do not.

#3. Passengers fairly often get the pick-up location wrong. If the move to pin on their app screen, they can get the location a mile or more off. Although they made the mistake, people in the wrong place blame Uber or GPS.

#4. Requesting a side trip through a fast food drive-thru. I allow this most of the time, but, if the line is long, I ask the PAX to go inside for their order because that's often faster.

#5. "Back seat driving." Sometimes a passenger will not want the driver to go the way the GPS navigation says to go. I am, as a rule, okay with that especially if they are used to a certain way of getting home. But it is a peeve if the PAX is simply too drunk to have the directions right.

#6. Extremely loud talking (really shouting). I must say that this peeve is almost exclusively an issue with female passengers who have had too much to drink. They talk over one another and, I suppose, try to make a point or be the funniest in the car. The decibels are up there with jet engines. And the distance from their bellowing mouths to the driver's sensitive ears (like mine) is less than three feet. I think this onerous behavior may stem from the fact that these loud mouths have come from a loud bar where they had to speak as if they were far away just to be heard.

#7. Pets as Pet Peeves. Uber drivers are required to accommodate "service animals." I am usually fine with all dogs, but once I got an old, bad smelling, and shedding, German Shepherd. Oh, that old dog shed a lot... took 10 minutes to get the hair out!

#8. Abuse of the rating system. I am a fan of the rating system when it is used in a fair and reasonable manner. That is, if a driver takes a pax from point A to point B in good time a correct distance, thus correct fare, then the rider should give the driver 5 stars. I routinely give my pax 5 stars just because the trip was uneventful and they were paying customers. But I have received less than perfect scores. Some people seem to have very high expectations and say that 4 means "good." Well, 4 is *not* good. If a driver falls below 4 on average, he, or she, is essentially on probation with Uber for an "improvement plan." The plan is to exceed a 4 star average on the next fifty trips, or that driver is kicked out of the app no longer a driver for Uber. In more than ten-thousand rides with Uber, my rating is above 4.9 stars, so I'm not worried about my rating status, but I am still peeved when I get a low mark. I get many laudable comments from the concert goers, now passengers going home.

One passenger rated me less than 5 and then took the time to explain that he or she felt my music had "too much base!" No, that was not something that was mentioned *while on the ride.*

I am very accommodating as to the music preferences of all my passengers. I often load Pandora with the band's station of the group that played at the concert from where I picked my passengers up. Many times they sing along with the favorites tunes of their favorite bands. I get great reviews for that.

Pet Peeves of Uber Passengers

Sometimes my PAX will follow up a comment on how nice, clean, warm, or pleasantly fragrant my car is with some disparagement of other Ubers they have had. Here's a short list of what they don't like:

#1. Smelly or unclean cars. Uber wants all drivers to keep their vehicles clean. I subscribe to a car wash service with unlimited number of washes and I do use a mild deodorizer that most passengers really like.

#2. New drivers that don't know the town and make mistakes navigating. I know how bad GPS can be sometimes, but generally it works. Also, when you do 13,000 rides as I have, the parts of town, bars, neighborhoods, businesses, and hotels are all in my head and very few mistakes are made.

#3. Smelly drivers! Come on people! Shower occasionally or regularly if you sweat a lot. I have more than a few passengers say that "drivers with B.O." is their pet peeve.

#4. Crazy, fast, or dangerous driving. Of course that is not a particularly bad trait of just Uber drivers. Taxicabs whose drivers don't own their cars are usually more careless in their driving habits than Ubers. In fact, Uber actually tracks drivers on their driving habits such as rapid acceleration of stopping that could indicate behavior that needs to be watched. They give drivers a daily report on the ratio of smooth acceleration and smooth stops compared to all acceleration and stops.

#5. Pickups that are cancelled because the driver can't find the passengers. I often hear that complaint, but that complaint really mystifies me. Why, when a passenger can be texted or called for clarification on the location, would a driver simply give up and cancel? Maybe it's just me, but I have never cancelled a trip because I couldn't find somebody. Usually, the passenger has given the wrong address, but that shouldn't result in cancellation if the driver simply contacts the rider.

Navigating Asheville

Many of my PAX have wondered how I manage to navigate around the city and countryside. Mostly they are from Florida or the Midwest where pretty much all the roads are in a grid often logically numbered and even given compass directions to aid in navigation. Here there are mountains, rivers, and twisting roads around and through them. It all seems confusing to visitors.

I tell them, "Well, first, I am from West Virginia. I grew up in this same mountain environment. Next, I say that GPS is usually reliable but I have learned most of my directions driving the past three years and 13,000 rides. I think Ubering actually improves memory. I guess that's a side-benefit of this job?"

A challenge to navigation that has nothing to do with topography is the fact that Asheville likes to name many streets the same with the small addition of "SE," "N," for relative location within the metropolitan area. Streets with the same name in different parts of town are differentiated with abbreviations such as "DR," "RD" and so on. I sometimes mistake, for example, Lookout Rd, for Lookout Dr. And sometimes my PAX put in the wrong one as their pick-up or drop-off point. Adding to the potential for confusion, is the changing name of essentially the same street.

As you approach Asheville on US 25, the five-lane Hendersonville Road becomes Biltmore Avenue which in a mile becomes Broadway Street which jogs to the left eventually merging straight ahead as Riverside Drive. Meanwhile, when US 25 ceases to be Broadway Street, the road becomes Merrimon Avenue. So you can start in Biltmore Village on Hendersonville Rd, then Biltmore Ave, then Broadway Street, then Merrimon Avenue without making a single turn!

Historically the different names for US 25 through Asheville used to have one just two names. From Pack Square south, the street was called "South Main Street;" and to the north, "North Main Street." That was apparently just way to simple a concept for the City Fathers a hundred years ago. If there had been some City Mothers at that time, the street naming craziness would not have happened.

Asheville Misnomers

Perhaps it's the old English teacher in me, but I find myself cringing as to incorrect diction manifest in the naming of roadways in and around Asheville. Some are correctly named; but more, it seems, are not so.

There is a road, yes *road* in West Asheville called "Johnston Boulevard." That road winds for a mile or two from Patton Avenue (a real avenue) to Johnston School Road (yes, a road). The definition of *boulevard* is "a wide and important street, tree lined, with trees often down the middle dividing the lanes." Johnston Boulevard has none of those attributes. It's Johnston Road and should be called that!

Asheville does have a boulevard. Its name is Broadway Street. Checking the definition, see above, Broadway is definitely a boulevard at least north of North Lexington Avenue.

The Oakley neighborhood in East Asheville also has a tiny side street, called "Main Street." I suppose that not-so-original name came up when Asheville's Main Street was renamed, Biltmore Avenue, Broadway

Street, and Merrimon Avenue. There is nothing "main" about Main Street" in Oakley. Oh, and nearby Main Street you can find a numbered street called "5th Avenue" which is not numbered for any particular reason, and does not meet the definition of an avenue.

One of my favorite misnomers for roadways is "College Street," a main thoroughfare through downtown Asheville. Many tourists ask where the college is. "About three miles north of here," I reply. There is no college on College Street. Also, going east on College Street, you come to a point just in front of the Beaucatcher Tunnel where College Street makes a sharp right turn. If you were to go straight you would be on Tunnel Road, aptly named for the tunnel you are about to go through. If you do stay on College Street, you will soon find yourself on a narrow winding road that meanders to the top of Beaucatcher Mountain. No longer a street, one wonders why not give that little road its own name, not just an extension of a downtown street that has no college?

Speaking of Tunnel Road, a five lane thoroughfare which goes all the way out to Swannanoa, NC, five miles east, there's another anomaly: At the Asheville Mall, someone decided that instead of an original name for the busy road that is a right turn from Tunnel Road and going downhill past the mall, they just called it "South Tunnel Road." It has nothing to do with the tunnel or US 70 East.

Other misnomers that either amuse or annoy me, or both, are the names of subdivisions and apartment complexes. A couple of miles from my house there is a subdivision of very large homes perched on steep lots on the side of a mountain. They call it "Hidden Valley." There is no valley there, but it is well-hidden on the side of a mountain!

A very large new apartment complex near to Biltmore Village is called, simply, "The District." But the place has no distinct features except for its massive size. I cannot understand why the developer chose such a non-descript name. It is close enough to the Village to evoke the locally powerful name Biltmore; it's on Fairview Road which would call for a name like "Fairview Residences." But no, The District sounds like a ghetto in a futuristic sci-fi novel.

"Biltmore" is so popular a name around here that the hospitality industry capitalizes on it without any qualms about the veracity of the names for their hotels. "Holiday Inn-Biltmore West," is actually in Candler, NC, six miles west of the Estate. "Holiday Inn-Biltmore East" is so far to the east (by six miles) of the Biltmore Estate to be technically in Swannanoa, NC.

Among the misnomers in the arsenal of local real estate marketers is one of my favorites: "The Reserve at Asheville." This large apartment complex must have lured tenants with its name. With a 28806 zip code, the apartments and town homes are in North Candler or South Leicester, ten miles northwest of downtown and well outside the City of Asheville.

Since Biltmore Village is a real and popular place with shops, restaurants, and hotels, suddenly, it seems, half of the new residential developments like to call themselves "village." I guess that is supposed to evoke small town hominess where everyone knows everyone and you can walk to shop, dine, or just walk you dog.

"Biltmore Park" is truly a village about 10 miles south of town. But there is no park at Biltmore Park. Many other "villages" are simply gated residential communities miles from restaurants, stores, and entertainment.

Clever Business Names

I love words. To pass the waiting time between rides; or waiting in lines at the store or DMV; or just when I have nothing better to do, I play Words with Friends™. I have played some game constantly with a friend in Houston since May 2011. My love for words, especially obscure ones also gives me an appreciation of puns and double entendres.

I have commented on the bad names; misleading names and outright false naming of places and roads around Asheville. To show that I am not always cranky and that I recognize and appreciate creativity with words where that is due, here is a short list of my personal favorite names of places in Asheville:

WRECK AMENDED (an automobile body shop)

HIP REPLACEMENTS (a clothing boutique)

RAG TIME (a vintage clothing store)

FOR EYES (optometry)

PLAY IT AGAIN (used sporting goods store)

PIZZA MIND (pizza, of course) And last but not

least: BUN INTENDED (a food truck)

Biltmore

The current Biltmore Estate encompasses the house, gardens, restaurants and hotels, and comprising *only* 7,000 acres of fields and forests. Much of the estate was beautifully landscaped out of the original 100,000 acres by Fredrick Law Olmstead the landscape architect of Central Park in New York City as well as many other parks. The estate is to this day is a working farm in addition to woodlands, trails, stables, and wedding venues.

As a working farm, Biltmore raises cattle, the feed for the cows, and has the single most visited winery in the USA. While they do also have vineyards, the best grapes processed there come shipped in from California.

The Biltmore House (1895), "The Largest Home in America" is a French styled chateau by the architect Richard Morris Hunt. It has 250 rooms and 43 bathrooms, an indoor swimming pool, and a bowling alley. There is a recent NY Times best-seller about the Biltmore House and Estate. *The Last Castle* by Denise Kiernan is a great read for anyone interested in Asheville and the Gilded Age in America.

I have taken many Uber trips to and from the house, gardens, hotels and winery on the Estate. By day the four mile trip in there is a scenic pleasure drive; by night it is part of Asheville's wild kingdom.

There are three negative aspects to Ubering to and from Biltmore. The first is the relatively low fares one gets for the trip. Many PAX from Biltmore only need to ride to downtown which means the fare is typically less than $8.00.

The second is that, in my experience, people going to and from the hotels and restaurants on the estate tend to be non-tippers. It is sort of galling to take well-to-do people to a $400 per night room, for a five-dollar ride that takes fifteen minutes and receive no tip at all. I think the well-off folks that can afford the hotel, and likely tip well at restaurants, seem oblivious to "taking care of" their driver.

The third issue regarding Biltmore is driving during the popular concerts help there in the summertime. Famous bands such as ZZ Top, Kool and the Gang, and the Commodores have played there. The crowds are enormous and Uber drivers get lots of requests for driving to and from them. There are frequent traffic jams on the winding one way roads and the net result is the fares are rarely worth the time it takes, especially after the concert. The Estate refuses to allow Uber drivers to pick passengers up in front of the house or near the concert venue. We must use the "Uber Pick-Up Area" which has changed several times, lately being in "Parking Lot C."

Still, I am glad to have all the business I can get, even for the Biltmore runs. The beauty of the place makes up for the negatives in doing ride shares in and out of there.

UberAir

Recently, Uber announced a "pilot program" (was the pun intended?) for helicopter service in major cities. It hasn't gotten off the ground yet, but it appears Uber is willing to invest millions in that service.

That announcement leaves the question of Uber's profitability, sort of, up in the air. As everyone knows, Uber has a very high value as a company. Estimates run to the neighborhood of $70 billion. That sky high worth seems odd when Uber claims losses in the hundreds of millions each year.

The high value of the company versus the claimed lack of profitability seems very odd to me and all the drivers I have talked to. After all, Uber has not invested in the millions of driver owned cars that are at the core of the business. Uber has invested millions in driverless cars due to the fact that their greatest expenditure is in the wages paid to drivers. But they get 20-25% of all fares and they also collect a set-up fee for every ride between one and two dollars per ride.

As to other costs, sure, they pay fees to Google for navigation, although they are attempting to develop their own navigation system. And they have a small army of attorneys to handle all sorts of litigation. Then there are the tech people who run the whole data rich app platform as well as the computers themselves. Still, one wonders how those billions of dollars in positive cash flow somehow elude profitability.

Back to "UberAir"—how would the ownership of a fleet of helicopters improve profitability? I guess that's a question for Dara Khosrowshahi, the new CEO who replaced the founder Travis Kalinsky. While Travis still sits on Uber's board, Dara is the new leader and visionary. He is committed to autonomous vehicle development but has had little to say about Uber Air or whether autonomous helicopters are also in Uber's future.

The same day I wrote the words above, Uber launched a video entitled "UberAir: It's Closer Than You Think." It's a very slick commercial featuring a young business woman getting home by taking an elevator to a helipad on the top of a skyscraper. She looks down at the grid-locked traffic, smiles, and is delivered to her suburban home in a matter of minutes.

Too Much of a Good Thing

Recently, New York and other major cities are attempting to limit the number of Uber and Lyft cars in their cities. The city councils have reacted to the fact of increased traffic attributed to the rideshare cars.

My take on that is to say the demand for such service means more supply of the service. But the City Fathers, have a point.

The fact is that people prefer to be taken closer to their destination than a bus or subway can. A couple of years ago, people didn't mind walking a couple of blocks to their offices after riding a bus, train, or subway.

Now those commuters either use Uber and Lyft exclusively, or they take a rideshare the last few blocks to their office. It is certainly worth the five buck ride especially if it is cold or rainy.

No doubt the cheapness of the service has created a problem. Too much of a good thing!

Uber Eats

One Uber service that is gaining in popularity is called "Uber Eats." It is a food delivery service sort of like take-out without the consumer needing to go out for the food. Meals or groceries are delivered by the same Uber drivers that normally take people to their destinations.

I tried this service as a provider of this service. Other drivers I have talked to say that it does increase their business and the tips are better in size and frequency. My own experience was not that good. In my first six trips picking up and delivering for Uber Eats, I received $30 in fees and got only one two dollar tip. All of that after parking, going in for food; then leaving, driving several miles, parking again, walking up several flights of apartment stairs and finally delivering the McDonald's burger and fries. "Thanks!" said the customers but five gave no tip!

In one period early in 2019, I was not driving for Uber or Lyft (see chapter *Fired!*) During the hiatus from driving, I tried some other food delivery gigs. For comparison, I'll talk about Grub Hub.

On a per hour basis, in my experience, GrubHub pays better per trip than

Uber or Lyft. It does not pay better per hour due to the less frequent opportunities. Grub Hub does pay way better than Uber Eats including tips. Tips with GrubHub are typically 100% of the fee pay! That is all due, I figured, to the way GrubHub's app works: The customer sees a screen that shows their cost of the food, the fee charged to them, and then asks for the customer to check a box either as percentage or fixed dollar amount as a tip. Uber Eats on the other hand works just as the rideshare app: the client rates the service after the delivery and then has to scroll down for the place to indicate a tip amount. See why Uber Eats tips are so puny compared to GrubHub?

I will have more to say about food delivery in my next book, *The Gig Economy: Inside Out.*

Uber Drivers as Employees?

One of the hotly debated issues surround Uber and Lyft is the pay and status of their drivers. In several large cities Uber and Lyft drivers went on strike (stopped working) to protest the lack of living wages, benefits and hours. I can certainly sympathize with those drivers try to make a living as drivers.

For my part, I like to part-time, work-when-you chose, aspects of this gig. As a "contractor," not an "employee," I have no schedule, no supervisor, and I can choose when to work or not at all. Of course, I am retired and have pensions and medicare.

California just passed a law that will require a minimum wage ($30 per hour is being floated). You can be certain that no driver would be free of scheduling, required shift hours, and other restrictions. I am definitely in favor of better pay, although the $20 per hour gross I currently get along with $.55/mile reduction of income for taxation is fine for now. So, I may be in a minority, but I am not in favor of employee status for rideshare drivers.

The Future of Uber

It is widely shown that the Uber ride sharing service has had a very positive impact on society in several ways. Several studies, for example, have shown that drunk driving arrests, DUI related accidents and fatalities have all significantly declined in cities where the service is available.

While that safety factor is dramatic and may be reason enough to love Uber, the bigger positive impact is not yet fully realized: The truly transformative nature of inexpensive ride sharing is that millions of people can now afford to get to work, school, shopping, or simply to recreational venues. Public transportation has always had the negative aspect of not taking people exactly where they need to go. Getting on a train or bus usually means long walks and long waits for service. Taxicabs are notoriously expensive. Ride sharing is cheap, dependable, and opens opportunity for jobs and other transportation needs that would simply not be accessible without ride-sharing.

I also have to add that retired persons (like me), or younger people needing a second job to augment low wages in other part-time jobs, can become Uber drivers and thus afford to live better lives. While there are no exact figures available, it is safe to say that various sources have put the number of Uber drivers in the USA at more than one million. It is hard to say how many more drive for Lyft especially since most drivers do so for both companies.

Uber sold its interests in the ride share business in China to a state supported company called Didi when that was Uber's second largest market. It was reported that Uber (or Travis Kalanick?) received $16 billion in that sale. But since then, Uber has done quite well in other markets. In India, for example, Uber has 400,000 drivers and is close to the size of its Indian rival Ola. Mexico City has become Uber's number one city market in terms of drivers, riders, and trips taken. In May 2017, Uber reported that it had completed five billion trips world-wide.

The growth of ride-sharing is likely to continue far into the future, not only in the current model with driver owned cars, but with autonomous vehicles, and perhaps with drones carrying well-heeled business people to those all-important meetings.

I would love to see a driverless Uber car navigating some of the unpaved, rutted, mountain roads that I encounter!

Uber and Out!

Made in the USA
Lexington, KY
30 November 2019

57851615R00109